WORKBOOK
to accompany

English words
from
Latin and Greek
elements

WORKBOOK

to accompany
the Second Edition of
DONALD M. AYERS'S

English words

from Latin and Greek elements

HELENA DETTMER
MARCIA LINDGREN

REVISED EDITION

THE UNIVERSITY OF ARIZONA PRESS
Tucson

About the Authors

HELENA DETTMER is a Professor in the Department of Classics at the University of Iowa. Before joining the faculty there, she obtained a B.A. degree with honors in Classics at Indiana University and earned M.A. and Ph.D. degrees at the University of Michigan. She served as President of the Classical Association of the Middle West and South in 1996–97. Dettmer served as chair of the Department of Classics from 1993 to 2001, as interim chair of the Department of French and Italian from 1998 to 1999, as founding Director of the Division of Interdisciplinary Programs from 2001 to 2005, and currently is serving as Associate Dean of Academic Programs and Services in the College of Liberal Arts and Sciences. She is the author of *Love by the Numbers: Form and Meaning in the Poetry of Catullus* (1997) and *Horace: A Study in Structure* (1983).

MARCIA LINDGREN earned a baccalaureate degree with honors from Southern Connecticut State University. She went on to graduate study in Classics at the University of Iowa, where she received her M.A. and Ph.D. degrees. In addition to teaching at Iowa, she served for ten years as an assistant to the Dean of the College of Liberal Arts and Sciences. She is currently an adjunct faculty member in the University of Iowa Department of Classics, where she also directs the Latin program.

THE UNIVERSITY OF ARIZONA PRESS
© 1986, 2005 The Arizona Board of Regents
All rights reserved.
First edition 1986.
Second edition 2005.

♾ This book is printed on acid-free, archival-quality paper.
Manufactured in the United States of America

16 15 14 13 12 11   7 6 5 4 3

ISBN 13: 978-0-8165-2318-4
ISBN 10: 0-8165-2318-5

The Laser Greek® font used to print the Greek letters in this work was produced by Linguist's Software, Inc., Edmonds, Washington.

FOR OUR CHILDREN

Heather, Michael, Anne, and Alex

David and Chris

CONTENTS

Part II: Word Elements from Greek

PREFACE TO THE REVISED EDITION

It has now been nearly twenty years since this workbook was first published as a companion to Donald M. Ayers's *English Words from Latin and Greek Elements*, revised by Thomas D. Worthen. The purpose of this updated version continues to be to give students practice with the Latin and Greek prefixes, bases, and suffixes introduced in the textbook and with English words derived from these elements.

Users familiar with the earlier edition of the workbook will note numerous changes and improvements and, we hope, wholeheartedly approve of them. The basic format remains the same. Each lesson contains a variety of exercises: short answer, matching, multiple choice, word analysis, fill-in-the-blanks, and true/false. Some of the exercises have been shortened and several entirely new exercises have been introduced, such as the dictionary exercise in Part I, Lesson V, and the word analysis exercises in Part I, Lessons IX and XVIII. Many of the true/false items have been replaced or revised, since we have found that these exercises often pose the greatest challenge for students. We also have taken this opportunity to revise or eliminate some items that have become dated or are likely to in the near future. In addition, we have made every attempt to be consistent and to improve the clarity of instructions for individual exercises, in some cases adding notes and providing sample answers. Finally, there is a new introduction for students with tips on how to get the most out of this workbook.

As we have revised the workbook, we have been mindful of all our constituents, not only students in college classrooms, but also high school students and independent learners of all ages. During the time since the workbook was first published there has been an explosion in accessibility to information of all kinds. Information about words and their history is now readily available as part of basic software packages and through the World Wide Web. This ready access to lexicons, thesauruses, and other resources has made it even easier for all of us to learn about etymology and to appreciate the power of words.

2005   Helena Dettmer and Marcia Lindgren

ACKNOWLEDGMENTS

We wish to thank our many students at the University of Iowa, who over the past four years have allowed us to test a great variety of exercises and who have provided us with numerous suggestions and comments. Professor Edward Schmoll and his students at the University of Missouri used a final edition of the workbook and shared their observations. Russell Clarke and Billie Anderson, graduate students in Classics at Iowa, assisted with word-processing. Ms. Anderson also provided assistance with the final proofreading, corrections, and modifications. Another graduate student, Joseph Hughes, often acted as a sounding board for specific items and general ideas. We also wish to thank R. L. Cherry for his many suggestions, both editorial and pedagogical. The authors are indebted to the Department of Classics of the University of Iowa for its support of this project.

1986   H. D. and M. L.

We are indebted to many people for their assistance with the revised edition of the workbook. Julie Van Dyke of the University of Iowa lent her considerable computer expertise to issues of layout and formatting. Donna Parsons of the Division of Interdisciplinary Programs and Amanda Barrett, a Classics graduate student, assisted with proofreading. We are grateful to Kathy Moon and Lisa Gray of the College of Liberal Arts and Sciences for their technical expertise. Thanks also are due to undergraduate honors student Lindsay Peterson, who took our revised edition for a test drive. We could not have completed this project without Classics graduate student Gwendolyn Gruber, who over the course of several years assisted with word-processing, final proofreading, and constructing a new answer key. Ms. Gruber also contributed numerous helpful suggestions for improvement in both form and content. We wish to thank the anonymous reviewers of an earlier draft for their excellent advice, which we have made every effort to incorporate into this edition. Patti Hartmann, Wayne Koch, Al Schroder, and Harrison Shaffer of the University of Arizona Press have provided valuable assistance with planning, production, and promotion of the workbook. We are especially grateful to our friend and colleague John Finamore, chair of the Department of Classics at Iowa, for his unfailing support and for allowing us to use his word-analysis exercises. Finally, the authors wish to acknowledge the support of College of Liberal Arts and Sciences, the Division of Interdisciplinary Programs, and the Department of Classics at the University of Iowa.

2005   H. D. and M. L.

TO THE TEACHER

The exercises in this workbook require brief responses and take a variety of forms, including short answer, matching, multiple choice, word analysis, fill-in-the-blanks, and true/false. The bases introduced in the textbook determine the number and types of exercises in each lesson: while some elements, particularly Latin verbal bases, have many English derivatives, others have few. The variety of exercises is intended to give teachers choices in supplementing their instruction. It is expected that few will wish to assign every exercise in every lesson.

It should be noted that Part II of the workbook (Word Elements from Greek) omits the scientific and medical bases introduced in Lessons XX-XXV. It was felt that the exercises in the textbook are more than adequate for these lessons, since in-depth study of scientific and medical terminology usually is reserved for a separate course.

Nearly every lesson in the workbook contains one or more exercises designed to provide further practice with elements learned in previous lessons. Major review sections occur periodically, and there is a comprehensive review at the end of Part I (Word Elements from Latin) and Part II (Word Elements from Greek). Latin review exercises also are included in Part II (Greek) to allow students to prepare for a comprehensive final examination or simply to refresh their knowledge of Latin elements. So that students may practice independently, answers to the major and comprehensive reviews are given in Appendix C.

The workbook should be used in conjunction with the exercises in *English Words from Latin and Greek Elements*. The exercises in the textbook present English words in sentences, while the workbook deals almost exclusively with words out of context. For this reason, the workbook can introduce a far greater number of words. Both experiences are important for students seeking to enrich their vocabularies.

We have found that the true/false and words of interest exercises provide an excellent basis for class discussion. But since these exercises often are the most challenging and time-consuming for students to do on their own, an instructor may wish to go over some or all of the material in class without demanding previous preparation. The Latin review exercises with topical themes (food, occupations, etc.) also may furnish possible subjects for class discussion.

Instructors are encouraged to adapt the workbook to their own needs. For example, a teacher could assign certain exercises and consider others optional, assign alternate items, use particular exercises as the basis for class discussion with or without previous preparation, use the workbook for independent study, or develop an effective correspondence course using the workbook in conjunction with the textbook. The pages of the workbook are perforated so that students may hand in homework.

The exercises in this workbook are intended to be fun as well as challenging. It is our hope that repeated practice with words derived from the Latin and Greek elements introduced in the textbook will serve as an effective tool that will enable students not only to build their vocabularies but also to develop a life-long fascination with the history of words.

TO THE STUDENT

Tips on How to Get the Most Out of This Book

In order to complete successfully the exercises in this workbook, you will need a standard college dictionary (such as the *American Heritage Dictionary*, *Merriam-Webster's Collegiate Dictionary*, or the *Random House Webster's College Dictionary*), in print or online.[*] On rare occasions you may need an unabridged dictionary to track down a word or etymology. Before you begin to do the exercises for any given lesson in the workbook, it is essential that you:

- Read the explanatory information at the beginning of the corresponding lesson in *English Words from Latin and Greek Elements*.

- Memorize the Latin or Greek **bases** (stems) introduced in each lesson along with their meanings (example: FIN-, end). Memorize any **prefixes** introduced in the lesson and their meanings (example: *circum*-, around). For **suffixes**, focus on learning the part of speech each suffix governs rather than memorizing its meaning (for example, -al, -ial, -eal is an adjective-forming suffix).

    It is strongly recommended that you make flashcards to help you learn all these word elements. Flashcards can help you memorize a large number of items quickly and efficiently, they can be organized into many different categories (by element type, by lesson, etc.), and they are useful for review, particularly before exams.

After memorizing the Latin or Greek elements and their meanings, turn to the exercises in the workbook and try to complete as many items as you can before consulting a dictionary or the textbook.

True/False Exercises
T/F questions in this workbook are based on information found either in the opening section of each lesson in *English Words from Latin and Greek Elements* or in the etymological section of a word entry in a dictionary (for example, [precarious < Lat. precarius, "obtained by prayer, uncertain"]). Note that the key word in most T/F questions appears in italics; this is the word you will need to look up to determine the correct answer. Some T/F questions have more than one key word.

Review Exercises
Nearly every lesson in the workbook contains several exercises clearly labeled **Review** that will give you further practice with information learned in previous lessons. In addition, there are periodic review sections covering five or more lessons (see pp. 41-44, for example) as well as comprehensive reviews for Part I (Word Elements from Latin) and Part II (Word Elements from Greek). After you have completed these optional exercises, you can check your own answers by referring to Appendix C at the back of the workbook.

---

[*] We recommend the following two dictionaries, which are available online without a subscription.
American Heritage Dictionary of the English Language: http://www.bartleby.com/am/
Merriam-Webster Online Dictionary: http://www.m-w.com/home.htm

PART I

WORD ELEMENTS FROM LATIN

INTRODUCTION & LESSON I

1. Indicate whether each statement is true or false by circling T or F.

T F   1. The Germanic and Latinate languages are the major contributors to the development of English.

T F   2. There is no recorded evidence of a Proto-Indo-European language.

T F   3. The English language has acquired the words *noodle*, *pretzel*, and *delicatessen* from German.

T F   4. Modern Greek is the single surviving representative of the Hellenic branch of the Indo-European family.

T F   5. Such words as *alchemy*, *algebra*, and *cipher* have entered the English language by way of the Moorish and Arabic cultures.

T F   6. The Roman occupation of Britain is reflected in the suffix -cester, -chester (Worcester, Dorchester), which derives from the Latin word for "camp."

T F   7. Ironically, English has borrowed no words from the languages of Native Americans.

T F   8. It is easy to determine whether a Latinate word in English derives directly from Latin or enters English through French.

T F   9. Most of the principal languages of Europe belong to the Indo-European family.

T F   10. Many Dutch words that have entered the English language are concerned with sailing and art.

T F   11. The Romance languages, the descendants of Latin, do not reflect the vastness of the empire Rome once held.

T F   12. Cognate languages derive from a common ancestor.

T F   13. The pronouns of Modern English bear little resemblance to those of Old English.

T F   14. The battle of Hastings in 1066 is an event of little consequence for the development of the English language.

T F   15. In Great Britain, the French spelling of some words (such as *colour* and *humour*) has been retained, while in the United States the spelling has reverted to Latin.

2. Dictionary. Indicate whether each statement is true or false by circling T or F.

(T) F   1. *Paraphernalia* once referred to property besides dowry that a bride brought to the home of her new husband.

T (F)   2. *Good humored* should be written as one word (goodhumored).

T (F)   3. The etymological meaning of *amethyst* is "remedy against drunkenness."

(T) F   4. *Antennae* is the only plural form of *antenna* acceptable in formal English.

T   F   5. The word *cayuse* is used chiefly in the western part of the United States.

(T) F   6. *Kerb* is the British spelling of the American *curb*.

T (F)   7. The primary accent of *chiropodist* falls on the second syllable.

(T) F   8. *Pub* is a shortened form of *public house*.

T (F)   9. The word *gerrymander* is a coinage that combines the name of a former governor of Massachusetts, Elbridge Gerry, with *salamander*.

T   F   10. The red condiment used by Americans to anoint hamburgers and French fries may be spelled *catchup, catsup,* or *ketchup*.

3. Dictionary. Match each word or symbol with the best definition.

_C_ 1. obsolete
_D_ 2. informal
_B_ 3. [ ]
_F_ 4. archaic
_A_ 5. ?
_E_ 6. <

A. symbol signifying "hypothetical" or "origin unknown"

B. symbols that enclose information about a word's origin

C. refers to a meaning no longer in use

D. language more appropriate for spoken use

E. symbol for "derives from"

F. refers to a meaning no longer in use except in special circumstances

4

LESSON II

1. Circle the letter of the best definition. Be sure that nouns are defined by nouns, verbs by verbs, and adjectives by adjectives. If you are unsure of your answer, consult a dictionary.*

   1. verbose: (A) wordy   (B) talkativeness   (C) to use too many words

   2. fortitude: (A) strong   (B) strength   (C) to strengthen

   3. divest: (A) stripped   (B) deprivation   (C) to strip or deprive of anything

   4. affirmation: (A) declaring assent   (B) a positive statement   (C) to state positively

   5. artificial: (A) produced by man   (B) something produced by man   (C) to contrive

   6. tripartite: (A) divided into three parts   (B) division into three parts
                  (C) to divide into three parts

   7. refinement: (A) cultivated   (B) elegance   (C) to make more elegant

   8. alienation: (A) strange   (B) estrangement   (C) to make hostile

   9. fortify: (A) strong   (B) strength   (C) to strengthen

  10. confirm: (A) firmly established   (B) proof   (C) to prove

  11. finale: (A) pertaining to the end   (B) conclusion   (C) to conclude

  12. aggrandize: (A) increased in size   (B) magnification   (C) to make great

  13. particularity: (A) specific   (B) a special characteristic   (C) to treat in detail

  14. linear: (A) arranged in a line   (B) division into lines   (C) to outline

  15. nullify: (A) invalid   (B) nothingness   (C) to invalidate

*Words may be composed of prefixes, bases, and suffixes. **Bases** contain the core meaning of the word. **Prefixes** may indicate direction (back, in, over, under, etc.), or they may negate or intensify the meaning of the base. **Suffixes** indicate part of speech (noun, verb, or adjective).

2. Words of Interest. Supply the appropriate word from the list below.

	Word	Etymological Meaning	Current Meaning
1.	_____	a burdening	grounds for complaint; resentment
2.	_____	rented land	land on which crops and livestock are raised
3.	_____	lacking skill	sluggish by habit or nature
4.	_____	reduction to nothing	total destruction
5.	_____	oily flax	a floor covering
6.	_____	divided or even game	danger
7.	_____	disguise	grotesque imitation
8.	_____	soft and loud tones	keyboard instrument in which hammers strike metal strings
9.	_____	cloth made of flax	intimate clothing worn by women
10.	_____	that which is firm or fixed	the heavens
11.	_____	work of art	trickery; cleverness
12.	_____	excessively concerned with fine points	fussy
13.	_____	byword	maxim; pithy saying
14.	_____	to settle a payment	to supply with capital
15.	_____	substance barely connected	waxy substance used in candles, etc.

annihilation	grandma	paraffin
artifice	grievance	pianoforte
farm	inert	proverb
finance	jeopardy	transvestite
finicky	lingerie	travesty
firmament	linoleum	trombone

3. <u>ART-; FIN-; FIRM-; FORT-; GRAND-; LINE-; NIHIL-; NUL(L)-; VERB-; VEST-</u>

Match each word with the best definition.

____ 1. artisan	A.	excessively large in scope
____ 2. definitive	B.	pertaining to words
____ 3. fine	C.	to furnish with power
____ 4. infirmary	D.	decisive
____ 5. fortress	E.	strong point
____ 6. forte	F.	a stronghold
____ 7. comfort	G.	ancestry
____ 8. grandiose	H.	sum of money exacted as a penalty
____ 9. delineate	I.	craftsman
____ 10. lineage	J.	to void
____ 11. nihilism	K.	to trace in outline
____ 12. annul	L.	small hospital
____ 13. verbal	M.	to give strength
____ 14. invest	N.	a place for keeping ceremonial garments
____ 15. vestry	O.	total rejection of traditional values

4. Indicate whether the following pairs are synonyms or antonyms by circling S or A.

S	A	1. gravity	-	solemnity
S	A	2. infinite	-	limited
S	A	3. finery	-	adornment
S	A	4. grandeur	-	magnificence
S	A	5. aggravate	-	improve
S	A	6. align	-	adjust
S	A	7. infirmity	-	healthiness
S	A	8. verbatim	-	literally
S	A	9. partisan	-	biased
S	A	10. alien	-	familiar
S	A	11. affinity	-	kinship
S	A	12. grievous	-	oppressive
S	A	13. artful	-	contrived
S	A	14. verbiage	-	wordiness
S	A	15. indefinite	-	certain

5. <u>PART-</u>

Match each word with the best definition.

____ 1. repartee	A. a trace; speck
____ 2. particle	B. to have a share
____ 3. impart	C. a package
____ 4. partake	D. a separate room or chamber
____ 5. parcel	E. a witty reply
____ 6. departure	F. a natural complement
____ 7. counterpart	G. the act of leaving
____ 8. participle	H. a social gathering
____ 9. compartment	I. a verbal adjective
____ 10. party	J. to bestow

LESSON III

1. Identify the prefix and base in each word and then give the meaning of each element. (Bases from Lesson II are included.)

	PREFIX	BASE
1. ad | vent	*to*	*come*
2. abjure		
3. deprecate		
4. affinity		
5. circumlocutory		
6. deduction		
7. contravene		
8. aggrandizement		
9. divest		
10. counterpart		
11. annulment		
12. collude		
13. departure		
14. abscess		
15. circumvent		
16. comfort		
17. abstruse		
18. antecedent		
19. confirm		
20. aggravation		

2. Words of Interest. Supply the appropriate word from the list below.

	Word	Etymological Meaning	Current Meaning
1.	_____	token that makes something come to mind	memento
2.	_____	that which the earth brings forth	fresh fruit and vegetables
3.	_____	belly-speaker	voice-thrower
4.	_____	removal of meat	Mardi Gras; festival
5.	_____	to lead out [a child]	to instruct
6.	_____	a wrong	damage; pain
7.	_____	thrust out of sight	difficult to understand
8.	_____	area over which an official speaks the law	authority to exercise control
9.	_____	one recently arrived	upstart
10.	_____	something about to happen	an undertaking involving risk
11.	_____	light of hand	trickery; deception
12.	_____	a coming together	assembly of witches
13.	_____	something raised	a pier
14.	_____	an interruption	conversation

abstruse	injury	levy
adventure	interlocution	parvenu
carnival	jurisdiction	produce
coven	legerdemain	souvenir
educate	levee	ventriloquist

3. Indicate whether the following pairs are synonyms or antonyms by circling S or A.

S	A	1. obloquy	-	abuse
S	A	2. obtrusive	-	inconspicuous
S	A	3. levity	-	gravity
S	A	4. prevent	-	hinder
S	A	5. alleviate	-	oppress
S	A	6. ludicrous	-	comical
S	A	7. deprecate	-	disapprove
S	A	8. contravene	-	oppose
S	A	9. adjust	-	arrange
S	A	10. conventional	-	original
S	A	11. intervene	-	meddle
S	A	12. colloquial	-	formal
S	A	13. irrelevant	-	pertinent
S	A	14. unproductive	-	prolific
S	A	15. imprecate	-	curse

4. <u>DUC-, DUCT-</u>

Match each word with the best definition.*

____ 1. abduction	A. subtraction
____ 2. conduct	B. sexual enticement
____ 3. deduction	C. something manufactured
____ 4. traducement	D. kidnapping
____ 5. inducement	E. installation into office
____ 6. induction	F. generation of offspring
____ 7. introduction	G. slander
____ 8. product	H. deportment, behavior
____ 9. seduction	I. preface
____ 10. reproduction	J. incentive

*The verbs that correspond to these nouns end in -duce or -duct: *abduct, conduct, deduct, induce, induct,* etc.

5. Indicate whether each statement is true or false by circling T or F.*

   T   F   1. *Somniloquists* talk in their sleep.

   T   F   2. The word *alibi* means that a person was "elsewhere" when the crime was committed.

   T   F   3. The etymological meaning of *null* is "not any."

   T   F   4. A *grievous* error is one of little consequence.

   T   F   5. The noun *decedent* is roughly equivalent to the euphemistic expression "to pass away."

   T   F   6. An *alienee* is a female extraterrestrial.

   T   F   7. *Paraffin* derives its name from its relative lack of affinity to other materials.

   T   F   8. Fort- in *fortnight* derives from the Latin base FORT-.

   T   F   9. *Hoosegow*, slang for "jail," ultimately derives from the Latin base JUDIC-.

   T   F   10. The etymology of *precarious* (depending on prayer) suggests the uncertain relationship that the Romans had with their gods, whereby praying was "risky" business.

*True/False questions are based on information found in the introductory section to each lesson of *English Words from Latin and Greek Elements* or on information found in the etymological section of a word entry in the dictionary (e.g., [*precarious* < Lat. *precarius*, "obtained by prayer, uncertain"]).

6. <u>LUD-, LUS-</u>

Match each word with the best definition.**

  ____ 1. allusion   A. conspiracy

  ____ 2. collusion   B. evasion

  ____ 3. delusion/illusion   C. indirect reference

  ____ 4. elusion   D. introduction

  ____ 5. prelude/prelusion   E. self-deception; deception

**The verbs that correspond to these nouns end in -lude: *allude, collude*, etc.; the adjectives end in -lusive or -lusory: *allusive, collusive, delusive* or *delusory*, etc.

12

7. <u>CED-, CESS-</u>

Match each word with the best definition.*

____ 1. access	A. superabundance
____ 2. antecedent	B. acknowledgment; subsidiary business
____ 3. concession	C. suspension of activities
____ 4. excess	D. a continuous, orderly movement of people or objects; parade
____ 5. intercession	
____ 6. precedent	E. forebear
____ 7. procession	F. achievement
____ 8. recess	G. prior example; model
____ 9. secession	H. approach
____ 10. success	I. formal withdrawal
	J. mediation

*With the exceptions of *access* and *recess*, the verbs that correspond to these nouns end in -cede or -ceed: *accede, antecede, concede, exceed,* etc.

8. <u>JUR-</u>

Match each word with the best definition.**

____ 1. abjure	A. to command solemnly
____ 2. adjure	B. to harm
____ 3. conjure	C. to recant; to renounce
____ 4. injure	D. to swear falsely under oath
____ 5. perjure	E. to summon by incantation

**The nouns that correspond to these verbs end in -juration or -jury: *abjuration, adjuration, conjuration, injury,* and *perjury*.

9. Review:* Indicate whether the following pairs are synonyms or antonyms by circling S or A.

S	A	1. definitive	-	inconclusive
S	A	2. judicious	-	sensible
S	A	3. inalienable	-	transferable
S	A	4. aggravate	-	worsen
S	A	5. annihilate	-	destroy
S	A	6. elevate	-	lower
S	A	7. success	-	failure
S	A	8. prejudiced	-	impartial
S	A	9. educated	-	knowledgeable
S	A	10. adjure	-	exhort
S	A	11. reduction	-	increment
S	A	12. alignment	-	adjustment

10. Review:* Match each word with the best definition.

____ 1. infirm	A. a share
____ 2. fort	B. invalidity
____ 3. investiture	C. contrivance
____ 4. refined	D. deep emotional distress
____ 5. grief	E. descent from a common ancestor
____ 6. portion	F. army post
____ 7. particle	G. "heavy with child": pregnant
____ 8. enforce	H. weak
____ 9. grand	I. positive; favoring
____ 10. nullity	J. the act of authorizing
____ 11. alienate	K. a very small portion
____ 12. lineage	L. to execute vigorously
____ 13. artifice	M. lavish; stately
____ 14. affirmative	N. purified; elegant
____ 15. gravid	O. to estrange

*All review exercises are optional and should be assigned at the discretion of the instructor.

LESSON IV

1. <u>GREG-</u>

Match each word with its <u>etymological</u> meaning.

____ 1. gregarious	A. a [spiritual] flock
____ 2. egregious	B. to keep from the flock
____ 3. aggregate	C. marked by a liking for the flock
____ 4. congregation	D. the sum of the flock
____ 5. segregate	E. standing out from the flock

2. <u>CRUC-; HAB-, AB-, (HIB-); PED-; PUNG-, PUNCT-; SACR-, (SECR-); SANCT-; SENT-, SENS-; TURB-; VI(A)-</u>

Match each word with the best definition.

____ 1. crucial	A. to make unnecessary
____ 2. excruciating	B. convenient and advantageous
____ 3. cohabit	C. to profane
____ 4. exhibition	D. the pricking of conscience
____ 5. impediment	E. hindrance
____ 6. expedient	F. going on foot; commonplace
____ 7. pedestrian	G. cloudy; confused
____ 8. punctuation	H. critically important
____ 9. compunction	I. to live together
____ 10. desecrate	J. agonizing
____ 11. sanctimonious	K. to respond emotionally to an indignity
____ 12. resent	L. public display
____ 13. sentimental	M. affectedly emotional
____ 14. turbid	N. hypocritically devout
____ 15. obviate	O. periods or commas, for example

3. Words of Interest. Supply the appropriate word from the list below.

	Word	Etymological Meaning	Current Meaning
1.	_____	off the beaten track	indirect; tricky
2.	_____	foot of a crane	genealogy
3.	_____	holy place	refuge
4.	_____	to mark out with dots	to delete
5.	_____	a stealing of sacred things	profanation
6.	_____	to sail across	to travel about
7.	_____	on the dot	prompt
8.	_____	intersection of three roads	insignificant matters
9.	_____	foot soldier	one earliest in a field of inquiry
10.	_____	a cross	critical point
11.	_____	a turning	personal account of something
12.	_____	to free the foot	to facilitate
13.	_____	doubly holy	inviolable
14.	_____	opinion	penalty
15.	_____	a small point	precise observance of formalities

cruise	expunge	sacrilege
crusade	pedigree	sacrosanct
crux	pioneer	sanctum
devious	prose	sentence
dishabille	punctilio	trivia
expedite	punctual	version

4. Indicate whether each statement is true or false by circling T or F.

T   F   1. An *inhibited* person is unlikely to apply for a job as an ecdysiast.

T   F   2. *Pedal* and its homophone *peddle* derive from the same Latin base.

T   F   3. People who speak in a *circumlocutory* manner get right to the point.

T   F   4. *Saint* ultimately derives from the base SANCT-.

T   F   5. *Sentiment* can mean "feeling" or "emotion."

T   F   6. *Reverberate* belongs to the VERB- family of words.

T   F   7. *Crucible* can refer to a severe, trying test.

T   F   8. *Viator* and *wayfarer* are synonyms.

T   F   9. A.D. (*anno Domini*) is an acronym.

T   F   10. The etymology of *sacrifice* is "to make [an offering to a deity] sacred."

5. <u>VERT-, VERS-</u>

Match each word with the best definition.*

____ 1. aversion	A.	a turning inward: withdrawal into oneself
____ 2. advertence	B.	regression
____ 3. animadversion	C.	dispute
____ 4. conversion	D.	distortion
____ 5. controversy	E.	severe, unjust criticism
____ 6. diversion	F.	the act of embracing a religious faith
____ 7. introversion	G.	the overturning of a government, for example
____ 8. perversion	H.	amusement
____ 9. reversion	I.	a turning of one's attention to something
____ 10. subversion	J.	a turning away from: repugnance

*The verbs that correspond to these nouns end in -vert: *avert*, *advert*, *animadvert*, etc.

6. Indicate whether the following pairs are synonyms or antonyms by circling S or A.

S	A	1. adversity	-	prosperity
S	A	2. assent	-	disagree
S	A	3. diverse	-	manifold
S	A	4. obvious	-	abstruse
S	A	5. habit	-	custom
S	A	6. perturbable	-	unruffled
S	A	7. sententious	-	pithy
S	A	8. versed	-	skilled
S	A	9. habitat	-	environment
S	A	10. versatile	-	unadaptable
S	A	11. execrable	-	detestable
S	A	12. invertebrate	-	weak
S	A	13. impervious	-	penetrable
S	A	14. adversary	-	foe
S	A	15. sanction	-	approve

7. The French Connection. The words in this exercise have entered English through French. Supply the appropriate word from the list below.

1. a regular customer   _____

2. from head to foot   _____

3. a literary postscript   _____

4. to call attention to a product   _____

5. very moving   _____

6. ailment; disorder   _____

7. dissolution of a marriage   _____

8. state of disorder   _____

9. travel by air or sea   _____

10. worry; inconvenience   _____

advertise	envoi	pied-à-terre
cap-a-pie	habitué	poignant
dishabille	malady	trouble
divorce	pedigree	voyage

8. Review: Supply the missing prefix or base.

1. seriousness   _ _ _ _ ity

2. weak; sickly   _ _ firm

3. word-for-word   _ _ _ _ atim

4. unfeeling   in _ _ _ _ itive

5. to strengthen   _ _ _ _ ify

6. to end   _ _ _ ish

7. to prick   _ _ _ _ _ ure

8. to reduce to nothing an _ _ _ _ _ ate

9. a go-between   _ _ _ _ _ cessor

10. holy   _ _ _ _ ed

11. talkative   l _ _ _ acious

12. limitless   _ _ finite

13. to clothe   v _ _ _

14. byword   _ _ _ verb

15. lightness   _ _ _ ity

16. cross-shaped   _ _ _ _ iform

17. by way of   v _ _

18. to lead away by force _ _ duct

19. foot of a statue   _ _ _ estal

20. to do wrong to   _ _ jure

9. Review: Circle the letter of the word that best fits the definition.

1. to escape:
   - (A) allude
   - (B) collude
   - (C) elude
   - (D) prelude

2. to force in:
   - (A) extrude
   - (B) intrude
   - (C) obtrude
   - (D) protrude

3. a decrease:
   - (A) induction
   - (B) reduction
   - (C) production
   - (D) seduction

4. to reject:
   - (A) abjure
   - (B) conjure
   - (C) adjure
   - (D) perjure

5. indefinable:
   - (A) allusive
   - (B) elusive
   - (C) delusive
   - (D) preclusive

6. to grant:
   - (A) concede
   - (B) proceed
   - (C) exceed
   - (D) recede

7. to subtract:
   - (A) abduct
   - (B) deduct
   - (C) conduct
   - (D) induct

8. a dislike:
   - (A) aversion
   - (B) reversion
   - (C) obversion
   - (D) subversion

9. to purify:
   - (A) confine
   - (B) fine
   - (C) define
   - (D) refine

10. to oppose:
    - (A) contravene
    - (B) intervene
    - (C) convene
    - (D) supervene

11. alluring:
    - (A) inductive
    - (B) reductive
    - (C) productive
    - (D) seductive

12. to elicit:
    - (A) adduce
    - (B) reduce
    - (C) educe
    - (D) traduce

13. upstart:
    - (A) avenue
    - (B) revenue
    - (C) parvenu
    - (D) venue

14. introductory:
    - (A) delusory
    - (B) ludicrous
    - (C) illusory
    - (D) prelusory

15. dialogue:
    - (A) colloquy
    - (B) obloquy
    - (C) elocution
    - (D) soliloquy

LESSON V

1. Give the unassimilated form of the prefix in each of the following words. Study the information in Appendix A before completing this exercise.

1. success	_sub_		10. correct	_____
2. assent	_____		11. approve	_____
3. impartial	_____		12. offer	_____
4. collude	_____		13. aggregate	_____
5. arrogant	_____		14. effort	_____
6. sufficient	_____		15. differ	_____
7. occurrence	_____		16. acquire	_____
8. illuminate	_____		17. supply	_____
9. affable	_____		18. irrevocable	_____

2. Indicate whether each statement is true or false by circling T or F.

T   F   1. The etymological meaning of *succor* is "to run to help."

T   F   2. A *digressive* style is characteristic of concise writing.

T   F   3. The etymological meaning of *preposterous* is "having the back part before [the rest]."

T   F   4. The life of a person living in a *cloister* is replete with social engagements.

T   F   5. Etymologically, a *pansy* is a "pensive"-looking flower.

T   F   6. An *egregious* error is one seldom detected.

T   F   7. *Curse* derives from the base CUR(R)-, CURS-.

T   F   8. A permit of entry from one country into another is called a *visa*.

T   F   9. *Poison,* like *poise,* belongs to the PEND-, PENS- family of words.

T   F   10. Etymologically, a *millipede* is a "thousand-footer."

Part I, Lesson V

3. Words of Interest. Supply the appropriate word from the list below.

	Word	Etymological Meaning	Current Meaning
1.	_____	likely to see visions	idealistic; impractical
2.	_____	something that enters into a mixture	component
3.	_____	a running	course of study
4.	_____	clear sight	intuitive insight
5.	_____	a list of words	words of a language
6.	_____	to admit to the next step	to receive a degree
7.	_____	looking all around	cautious
8.	_____	to look upon maliciously	to begrudge; to covet
9.	_____	foresighted	judicious
10.	_____	something weighed	a Mexican coin
11.	_____	observation of birds	protection; support
12.	_____	a pausing to look back	interval of relief
13.	_____	a filling out	an obscenity
14.	_____	place where medicine is weighed out	free clinic
15.	_____	runner	messenger

auspices
circumspect
clairvoyance
courier
curriculum
dispensary

distillery
envy
expletive
graduate
ingredient
peso

prudent
respite
specie
spice
visionary
vocabulary

22

4. In the following three exercises, match each word with the best definition.

CLUD-, CLUS-*

____ 1. conclude	A. to prevent; to make impossible
____ 2. exclude	B. to finish
____ 3. include	C. to place in solitude; to isolate
____ 4. occlude	D. to shut out
____ 5. preclude	E. to bring cusps of upper and lower teeth
____ 6. seclude	into alignment
	F. to be made up of; to contain

*The nouns that correspond to these verbs end in -clusion: *conclusion, exclusion*, etc. The adjectives end in -clusive: *conclusive, exclusive*, etc.

CLOS-**

____ 1. close	A. to surround
____ 2. disclose	B. to shut; to conclude
____ 3. enclose	C. to deprive of the right to renew
____ 4. foreclose	mortgaged property
	D. to reveal

**The nouns that correspond to these verbs end in -closure: *closure, disclosure*, etc.

VOC-, VOK-***

____ 1. advocate	A. to call together
____ 2. convoke	B. to call on for assistance; to solicit
____ 3. equivocate	C. to speak evasively
____ 4. evoke	D. to rescind
____ 5. invoke	E. to call forth
____ 6. provoke	F. to support verbally
____ 7. revoke	G. to incite

***The nouns that correspond to these verbs end in -vocation: *advocation, convocation*, etc.

5. Supply the missing prefix or base.

1. to oversee   _ _ _ _ _ vise

2. forerunner   pre _ _ _ _ or

3. incapable of being seen   in _ _ _ ible

4. a calling   _ _ _ ation

5. to pay out   _ _ pend

6. sight   _ _ _ ion

7. step by step   _ _ _ _ ual

8. to wave   _ _ _ ulate

9. payment   com _ _ _ _ ation

10. looking backward   _ _ _ _ _ spective

11. to look down upon   _ _ spise

12. unrehearsed performance impro _ _ _ ation

6. <u>GRAD-, GRESS-</u>

Match each word with the best definition.*

  ____ 1. aggression   A. return; reversion

  ____ 2. digression   B. exit

  ____ 3. egress or egression C. sin; infringement

  ____ 4. ingress or ingression D. forward movement

  ____ 5. progress or progression E. entry

  ____ 6. regress or regression F. hostility; offensive act

  ____ 7. transgression   G. deviation from the topic at hand

*The verbs that correspond to these nouns end in -gress: *aggress*, *digress*, etc. The adjectives end in -gressive: *aggressive*, *digressive*, etc.

7. Indicate whether the following pairs are synonyms or antonyms by circling S or A.

S	A	1. deplete	-	fill
S	A	2. cursory	-	hasty
S	A	3. suspicious	-	questionable
S	A	4. degrade	-	promote
S	A	5. redundant	-	deficient
S	A	6. speculate	-	conjecture
S	A	7. implement	-	perform
S	A	8. inspect	-	scrutinize
S	A	9. inconclusive	-	final
S	A	10. abundant	-	plentiful
S	A	11. suspend	-	delay
S	A	12. congress	-	convention
S	A	13. special	-	ordinary
S	A	14. vociferous	-	soft-spoken
S	A	15. append	-	attach

8. The French Connection. The words in this exercise have entered English through French. Supply the appropriate word from the list below.

1. ornamented by a different material _____

2. a step or stage in a course or process _____

3. pirate _____

4. small room for storage _____

5. to appraise (a situation) _____

6. a strong liking _____

7. to declare openly _____

8. a very small amount _____

9. achievement _____

10. to refill _____

11. pun   _____

12. to result; to contribute   _____

13. a style of enamelware   _____

14. in relation to; compared with   _____

15. passage connecting parts of a building   _____

accomplishment	corridor	redound
appliquéd	corsair	replenish
avow	degree	soupçon
cloisonné	equivoque	survey
closet	penchant	vis-à-vis

9. Review: Circle the letter of the word that is dissimilar in meaning from the other two.

1. (A) equivocation
   (B) compendium
   (C) conspectus

2. (A) advert
   (B) allude
   (C) espy

3. (A) dispense
   (B) apportion
   (C) expedite

4. (A) verbose
   (B) recessive
   (C) redundant

5. (A) evident
   (B) subversive
   (C) conspicuous

6. (A) pedigree
   (B) alignment
   (C) ancestry

7. (A) occurrence
   (B) event
   (C) coven

8. (A) precursor
   (B) courier
   (C) antecedent

9. (A) obviate
   (B) prevent
   (C) suspend

10. (A) definitive
    (B) recurrent
    (C) conclusive

11. (A) obloquy
    (B) colloquy
    (C) conversation

12. (A) educible
    (B) breviloquent
    (C) compendious

13. (A) completion
    (B) close
    (C) subvention

14. (A) annul
    (B) revoke
    (C) execrate

15. (A) special
    (B) particular
    (C) prosaic

16. (A) vouch
    (B) vilipend
    (C) despise

10. Review: Match each word with the best definition.

____ 1. excursion	A. a feeling about the future
____ 2. invidious	B. moving backward
____ 3. proverbial	C. remorse
____ 4. traverse	D. upset; alarmed
____ 5. interlinear	E. a shy person
____ 6. reproduce	F. a brief trip
____ 7. congregate	G. inserted between lines
____ 8. supervene	H. to distress
____ 9. perturbed	I. to withdraw formally
____ 10. secede	J. to assemble
____ 11. introvert	K. distorted
____ 12. aggrieve	L. a person who takes part in a dialogue
____ 13. presentiment	M. tending to cause resentment
____ 14. interlocutor	N. characteristic of a short, popular saying
____ 15. compunction	O. to occur as something additional
	P. to pass through
	Q. to bring forth again

11. Review: The French Connection. The words in this exercise have entered English through French. Match each word with the base from which it derives.

____	1. subdue	A. CED-, CESS-
____	2. visa	B. DUC-, DUCT-
____	3. appoint	C. FIN-
____	4. avenue	D. FORT-
____	5. abound	E. GRAV-
____	6. deceased	F. LEV-
____	7. enforce	G. LINE-
____	8. lingerie	H. PART-
____	9. parcel	I. PUNG-, PUNCT-
____	10. relieve	J. UND-
____	11. grief	K. VEN-, VENT-
____	12. financier	L. VID-, VIS-

12. Review: Dictionary. Circle the letter of the answer that best completes each statement, based on the following dictionary entry.

quaint, *adj.* 1. strange, peculiar in an interesting or amusing way. 2. oddly picturesque. 3. cleverly made. 4. *Archaic.* wise, skilled. 5. *Obs.* sly, crafty. [ME *queinte* < OF, var. of *cointe* clever, pleasing << L. *cognitus* known].

1. The earliest language from which the word evolves is:
   (A) Latin   (B) Old French   (C) Middle English   (D) none of the above

2. The part of speech of the word is:
   (A) noun   (B) adverb   (C) adjective   (D) verb

3. The archaic meaning of the word is:
   (A) wise   (B) peculiar   (C) oddly picturesque   (D) cleverly made

4. The obsolete meaning of the word is:
   (A) strange   (B) oddly picturesque   (C) wise   (D) sly

5. The word passed into English from:
   (A) Latin   (B) Old French   (C) Middle English   (D) none of the above

LESSON VI

1. Match each word with the best definition.

____ 1. bipartite	A. an introductory book
____ 2. quincunx	B. any group of seven
____ 3. primer	C. college administrator
____ 4. dub	D. pit where stone is excavated
____ 5. quarry	E. having two parts
____ 6. duplicity	F. a person of eighty years
____ 7. octogenarian	G. to furnish with a new sound track
____ 8. septet	H. framework for growing vines
____ 9. trellis	I. deceit
____ 10. dean	J. arrangement of five objects in a square or rectangle

2. Identify the numerical base in each word and then give the meanings of the bases.

1. century   _CENT-   hundred_____

2. combine   _____

3. decimate   _____

4. deuce   _____

5. mill   _____

6. octave   _____

7. prince   _____

8. quarter   _____

9. semiannual   _____

10. squadron   _____

3. Words of Interest. Supply the appropriate word from the list below.

	Word	Etymological Meaning	Current Meaning
1.	_____	nine each	devotion lasting nine days
2.	_____	a thousand paces	unit of length equaling 5280 feet
3.	_____	three-footed support	metal stand with short feet, placed under a hot dish
4.	_____	a foot and a half long	very long (used of words)
5.	_____	seventh month of early Roman calendar	ninth month of current calendar
6.	_____	a turning as one	cosmos
7.	_____	the ninth hour	midday
8.	_____	a period of 40 days	isolation imposed to stop the spread of disease
9.	_____	the sixth hour	an afternoon nap
10.	_____	a single pearl	a bulb vegetable
11.	_____	two scale pans	poise; equilibrium
12.	_____	one of a kind	single; incomparable
13.	_____	fifth essence	the most perfect embodiment [of]
14.	_____	a period of six months	half of an academic year
15.	_____	of two minds	doubtful

balance	novena	sesquipedalian
centurion	onion	siesta
dubious	quarantine	travail
July	quintessence	trivet
mile	semester	unique
noon	September	universe

4. Review: Write the following numbers in Arabic numerals.

1. LXI _____   4. liv _____
2. XXIV _____   5. MLXVI _____
3. DCCCIV _____   6. xciii _____

5. Review: Match each prefix with the best definition.

_____ 1. ad-   A. under; secretly

_____ 2. circum-   B. apart; in different directions, not

_____ 3. dis-   C. around

_____ 4. extra-   D. back; again

_____ 5. per-   E. after

_____ 6. re-   F. outside; beyond

_____ 7. sub-   G. to; toward

                    H. through; wrongly; completely

                    I. above; over

                    J. out; from

6. Review: Use a check to indicate which of the following prefixes do <u>not</u> undergo assimilation.

_____ 1. ab-   _____ 6. ob-

_____ 2. con-   _____ 7. per-

_____ 3. dis-   _____ 8. pre-

_____ 4. ex-   _____ 9. sub-

_____ 5. inter-   _____ 10. ultra-

7. Review: Use a check to indicate which of the following prefixes can mean "not."

_____ 1. ab-   _____ 4. in-

_____ 2. circum-   _____ 5. non-

_____ 3. dis-   _____ 6. per-

8. Review: Use a check to indicate which of the following prefixes can act as intensifiers. (Intensifying prefixes have the force of "very," "completely," "thoroughly," etc.)

_____ 1. ad-   _____ 6. ob-

_____ 2. con-   _____ 7. per-

_____ 3. de-   _____ 8. pre-

_____ 4. ex-   _____ 9. sub-

_____ 5. inter-   _____10. ultra-

9. Review: Indicate whether each statement is true or false by circling T or F.

T   F   1. "Heads" and "tails" refer to the *obverse* and *reverse* sides of a coin.

T   F   2. The Romans invented the punishment *decimation* to discourage mutiny in the ranks of the army.

T   F   3. An *alienist* deals with persons exhibiting aberrant behavior.

T   F   4. The words *compliment* and *complement* derive from different Latin bases.

T   F   5. To speak *vociferously* is to speak softly.

T   F   6. *Lingerie* once referred to linen goods in general.

T   F   7. *Pedestrian* has come to mean "commonplace" because formerly those who walked were persons of low social status.

T   F   8. The etymology of *travel* is "to labor."

T   F   9. Etymologically, *biscuit* and *zwieback* mean the same thing.

T   F   10. In English words, when the prefix ex- precedes a base beginning with s, the s drops out (for example, *execrate*, *expect*).

10. Review: Circle the letter of the word that best fits the definition.

1. to call upon:
   (A) convoke
   (B) invoke
   (C) provoke
   (D) revoke

2. thoughtful:
   (A) compendious
   (B) expensive
   (C) pendent
   (D) pensive

3. to bring on oneself:
   (A) concur
   (B) incur
   (C) occur
   (D) recur

4. ambiguous:
   (A) equivocal
   (B) provocative
   (C) vocalic
   (D) vociferous

5. to corrupt:
   (A) avert
   (B) divert
   (C) pervert
   (D) revert

6. attack:
   (A) aggression
   (B) digression
   (C) regression
   (D) transgression

7. to shut out:
   (A) conclude
   (B) exclude
   (C) include
   (D) preclude

8. hobby:
   (A) avocation
   (B) convocation
   (C) equivocation
   (D) invocation

9. to empty:
   (A) complete
   (B) deplete
   (C) implement
   (D) replete

10. pastime:
    (A) diversion
    (B) reversion
    (C) inversion
    (D) subversion

11. to separate:
    (A) aggregate
    (B) congregate
    (C) desegregate
    (D) segregate

12. subtraction:
    (A) adduction
    (B) deduction
    (C) production
    (D) seduction

13. evasive:
    (A) circumlocutory
    (B) colloquial
    (C) eloquent
    (D) loquacious

14. conversation:
    (A) concourse
    (B) course
    (C) discourse
    (D) recourse

15. to add:
    (A) append
    (B) expend
    (C) impend
    (D) suspend

16. secret agreement:
(A) collusion   (C) elusion
(B) delusion   (D) prolusion

17. to lie under oath:
(A) abjure   (C) conjure
(B) adjure   (D) perjure

18. consecutive:
(A) concessive   (C) recessive
(B) excessive   (D) successive

19. to oppose:
(A) contravene   (C) intervene
(B) convene   (D) supervene

20. to disagree:
(A) assent   (C) present
(B) dissent   (D) resent

11. Review: Words with Religious Associations. Match each word with the base from which it derives.

____ 1. vow	A. CANT-, (CENT-), [CHANT-]
____ 2. saint	B. CED-, CESS-
____ 3. convent	C. CLUD-, CLUS-, [CLOS-]
____ 4. habit	D. CRUC-
____ 5. crusade	E. HAB-, AB-, (HIB-)
____ 6. vestment	F. NOVEM-
____ 7. novena	G. PEND-, PENS-
____ 8. auspices	H. PRIM-
____ 9. Sistine	I. SANCT-
____ 10. cloister	J. SEXT-
____ 11. vision	K. SPEC-, (SPIC-), SPECT-
____ 12. dispensation	L. VEN-, VENT-
____ 13. chant	M. VEST-
____ 14. processional	N. VID-, VIS-
____ 15. prioress	O. VOC-, VOK-

LESSON VII

1. Try to supply the appropriate word before referring to the list of possible answers below.

1. Tumors generally are classified as either _____ or _____.
   The one is "kindly," the other cancerous.

2. A person "without care" is _____.

3. A person who can write or speak many languages is _____.

4. The adjective _____ means "without life" or "lifeless."

5. The adjective _____ etymologically means "to be of one mind."

6. A person wishing others well or good might be described as _____;
   a person wishing others evil, on the other hand, might be described as
   _____.

7. The noun _____ etymologically means "the turning of a year."

8. A person authorized to act for another is called a _____.

9. Plants that live from year to year are called _____; plants that live for
   one year only are called _____.

10. The adjective _____ etymologically means possessing "a noble
    (great) spirit."

11. The noun _____ refers to yearly payments of income.

12. A _____ pretends to be sick in order to avoid work or other
    commitments.

anniversary	inanimate	multilingual
annuals	magnanimous	perennials
annuities	malevolent	proxy
benevolent	malignant	secure
benign	malingerer	unanimous

2. <u>ANIM-; BENE-, BON-; CANT-, (CENT-); CUR-; EQU-, (IQU-); MAGN-; MAL(E)-; MULT-</u>

Match each word with the best definition.

____ 1. animate	A. to stress; to emphasize
____ 2. animalcule	B. "big shot"
____ 3. beneficial	C. having great variety
____ 4. embellish	D. an amoeba, for example
____ 5. accentuate	E. a job requiring little or no work
____ 6. sinecure	F. spiteful
____ 7. accuracy	G. to supervise an examination
____ 8. proctor (v.)	H. advantageous
____ 9. adequate	I. an object causing attraction
____ 10. equilibrium	J. bombastic speech
____ 11. magnate	K. genuine; lacking pretense
____ 12. magniloquence	L. to enhance with ornamental details
____ 13. malicious	M. exactness
____ 14. multiculturalism	N. balance
____ 15. multifarious	O. to enliven
	P. sufficient
	Q. a social theory that encourages interest in many cultures

3. Indicate whether each statement is true or false by circling T or F.

T   F   1. The etymology of *canary* is "melodious songster."

T   F   2. *Magnum*, as in "a magnum of champagne," derives from the base MAGN-.

T   F   3. The etymological meaning of *incentive* is "that which sets the tune," and hence incites to action.

T   F   4. *Equine* belongs to the EQU-, (IQU-) family of words.

T   F   5. A *bon mot* is a particularly inappropriate word or expression.

T   F   6. The *magnolia* derives its name from its large flowers.

T   F   7. If a person is *disenchanted*, "the spell has worn off."

T   F   8. Originally, *bonanza* meant "calm sea."

T   F   9. The etymological meaning of *debonair* is "of good lineage."

T   F   10. An archaic meaning of *curious* is "accomplished with skill."

4. PLIC-, PLEX-, [-PLY]

Supply the appropriate word from the list below.

1. to answer

    _____

2. easily bent; flexible

    _____

3. deception

    _____

4. to make many or manifold

    _____

5. a fold in clothing

    _____

6. any combination of three

    _____

7. partner in crime

    _____

8. the appearance and color of a person's skin, especially the face

    _____

9. to puzzle; to bewilder

    _____

10. incapable of being explained

    _____

11. to indicate indirectly

    _____

12. a person who hires someone for wages

    _____

13. to use selfishly; to take advantage of

    _____

14. a copy; reproduction

    _____

15. tangled; involved

    _____

accomplice	exploit	pleat
complex	imply	pliable
complexion	inexplicable	replica
duplicity	multiply	reply
employer	perplex	triplet

5. FER-

Match each word with the best definition.

____ 1. circumference	A. a meeting for consultation
____ 2. conference	B. absence of interest
____ 3. deference	C. the favoring of one over another
____ 4. difference	D. perimeter
____ 5. indifference	E. a mention; footnote
____ 6. inference	F. logical conclusion from evidence
____ 7. preference	G. removal from one place to another
____ 8. reference	H. submission to opinion of another
____ 9. sufferance	I. dissimilarity
____ 10. transference	J. capacity to endure hardship

6. LAT-

Match each word with the best definition.*

____ 1. collate	A. to fill with joy
____ 2. correlate	B. to carry over into another language
____ 3. elate	C. to bring into mutual relation
____ 4. relate	D. to assemble pages of a document in their proper order
____ 5. translate	E. to tell

*The nouns that correspond to these verbs end in -lation: *collation*, *correlation*, etc.

7. Circle the letter of the word that best completes each statement.

1. A synonym for *retraction* that means "a singing back" is: (A) chanson (B) dirge (C) recantation

2. A substance that brings or yields a fragrant odor is described as: (A) pungent (B) odoriferous (C) malodorous

3. A person who usually looks on the bright side is a(n): (A) optimist (B) opportunist (C) beneficiary

4. A synonym for *genuine* that in Latin means "in good faith" is: (A) de facto (B) bona fide (C) ipsissima verba

5. An object whose value derives from its rarity or unusualness is called a: (A) sui generis (B) magnifico (C) curio

6. A synonym for *composure* that means "evenness of mind" is: (A) equanimity (B) equivocation (C) pusillanimity

7. A word describing a history of events in successive years is: (A) narrative (B) annals (C) excerpts

8. Another word for *rooster* that means "clear singer" is: (A) capon (B) cock (C) chanticleer

8. Review: Form the antonym of each word by substituting another prefix. Remember assimilation (see Appendix A).

1. antebellum _____ bellum

2. repletion _____ pletion

3. dissent _____ sent

4. explicit _____ plicit

5. progress _____ gress

6. consecrate _____ secrate

7. recede _____ ceed

8. divest _____ vest

9. introverted _____ verted

10. inhibit _____ hibit

9. Review: The following words have entered English through Italian or Spanish. From the list below, supply the base from which each word derives.

<u>Italian</u>

1. punctilio　＿＿＿＿＿＿＿＿
2. magnifico　＿＿＿＿＿＿＿＿
3. vista　＿＿＿＿＿＿＿＿
4. malaria　＿＿＿＿＿＿＿＿
5. belladonna　＿＿＿＿＿＿＿＿
6. fortissimo　＿＿＿＿＿＿＿＿
7. finale　＿＿＿＿＿＿＿＿
8. piedmont　＿＿＿＿＿＿＿＿
9. grandioso　＿＿＿＿＿＿＿＿
10. pococurante　＿＿＿＿＿＿＿＿
11. squadron　＿＿＿＿＿＿＿＿
12. canto　＿＿＿＿＿＿＿＿
13. duce　＿＿＿＿＿＿＿＿
14. replica　＿＿＿＿＿＿＿＿

<u>Spanish</u>

1. corral　＿＿＿＿＿＿＿＿
2. siesta　＿＿＿＿＿＿＿＿
3. peon　＿＿＿＿＿＿＿＿
4. bonanza　＿＿＿＿＿＿＿＿
5. crusade　＿＿＿＿＿＿＿＿
6. doubloon　＿＿＿＿＿＿＿＿
7. peso　＿＿＿＿＿＿＿＿
8. grandee　＿＿＿＿＿＿＿＿

BENE-, BON-	FIN-	PLIC-, PLEX-
CANT-, (CENT-)	FORT-	PUNG-, PUNCT-
CRUC-	GRAND-	QUADR(U)-
CUR-	MAGN-	SEXT-
CUR(R)-, CURS-	MAL(E)-	VID-, VIS-
DU-	PED-	
DUC-, DUCT-	PEND-, PENS-	

REVIEW OF LESSONS II–VII (SELF-TESTING: Answers can be found in Appendix C.)

1. Give the unassimilated form of the prefix in each of the following words.

1. annihilate	_____	6. imprecation	_____
2. succor	_____	7. aggrandize	_____
3. compunction	_____	8. illusion	_____
4. effort	_____	9. occlude	_____
5. different	_____	10. suppliant	_____

2. Supply the appropriate prefix. Remember assimilation.

1. to look down (on)	_____	spise
2. to keep from the flock; to isolate	_____	gregate
3. to lead away; to kidnap	_____	duct
4. a going forward	_____	gress
5. looking all around	_____	spect
6. afterword	_____	script
7. turned outward (outside)	_____	verted
8. between the lines	_____	linear
9. a coming to; arrival	_____	vent
10. to turn a marriage contract asunder	_____	vorce
11. to oversee	_____	vise
12. a speaking together; conference	_____	loquy
13. turned inward (within)	_____	verted
14. an overstepping of bounds	_____	gression
15. allowing passage through	_____	vious

3. Calendar. Supply the appropriate month from the list below.

1. Month named after the goddess of marriage   _____

2. Month named after the Roman god of war   _____

3. Originally, the tenth month in the Roman calendar   _____

4. Month named after the Roman god with two faces   _____

5. Month named after the Latin word which signifies the "opening" of buds   _____

6. Month named for a purification festival   _____

7. Originally, the eighth month in the Roman calendar   _____

8. Month named after Julius Caesar   _____

9. Originally, the seventh month in the Roman calendar   _____

10. Month named after Augustus Caesar   _____

January	May	September
February	June	October
March	July	November
April	August	December

4. Match each word with the best definition.

____	1. pliable	A.	to live from season to season
____	2. gravamen	B.	composed; dignified
____	3. turbulent	C.	tempestuous
____	4. ability	D.	flexible
____	5. bonus	E.	asymmetric
____	6. poised	F.	to declare; to utter
____	7. voice	G.	talent
____	8. sensational	H.	exciting; spectacular
____	9. disproportionate	I.	reward
____	10. perennate	J.	weightiest part of an accusation

5. Supply the missing base.

1. first   _ _ _ _ ary

2. speech spoken alone   soli _ _ _ _ y

3. oneness   _ _ ity

4. to wrong   in _ _ _ e

5. every two years   bi _ _ _ _ al

6. a calling   _ _ _ ation

7. to estrange   _ _ _ _ _ ate

8. twosome   _ _ o

9. evildoer   _ _ _ _ factor

10. to take part   _ _ _ _ icipate

11. wordiness   _ _ _ _ osity

12. the many   _ _ _ _ itude

13. person on foot   _ _ _ estrian

14. holiness   _ _ _ _ _ ity

15. greatness in size   _ _ _ _ itude

16. feeling   _ _ _ _ ation

17. hanging   _ _ _ _ ent

18. fullness   _ _ _ _ ty

19. lively   _ _ _ _ ated

20. a spell   in _ _ _ _ ation

6. Indicate the correct answer by circling A or B.

1. main:	(A) principal	(B) principle
2. prudent:	(A) judicial	(B) judicious
3. stinging:	(A) punctilious	(B) pungent
4. wickedness:	(A) inequity	(B) iniquity
5. passport:	(A) vista	(B) visa
6. clear:	(A) perspicacious	(B) perspicuous
7. a yielding:	(A) cession	(B) session
8. fondness:	(A) penchant	(B) pendant
9. savage:	(A) primeval	(B) primitive
10. dangerous:	(A) precarious	(B) precatory
11. conclusive:	(A) definite	(B) definitive
12. weakness:	(A) infirmity	(B) infirmary

7. Indicate whether the following pairs are synonyms or antonyms by circling S or A.

S	A	1. proviso	-	stipulation
S	A	2. abstruse	-	evident
S	A	3. revenant	-	ghost
S	A	4. perturbable	-	serene
S	A	5. circumvent	-	bypass
S	A	6. replenish	-	empty
S	A	7. induction	-	initiation
S	A	8. deprecate	-	approve
S	A	9. traduce	-	malign
S	A	10. curious	-	meddlesome
S	A	11. inhabit	-	dwell
S	A	12. provenance	-	origin
S	A	13. inundate	-	flood
S	A	14. relieve	-	oppress
S	A	15. pedigree	-	lineage

LESSON VIII

1. Indicate whether the following pairs are synonyms or antonyms by circling S or A.

S	A	1. temporary	-	transient
S	A	2. corporeal	-	spiritual
S	A	3. simulate	-	counterfeit
S	A	4. tense	-	strained
S	A	5. dissembler	-	hypocrite
S	A	6. aquatic	-	terrestrial
S	A	7. omnivorous	-	finicky
S	A	8. extemporaneous	-	improvised
S	A	9. corpulent	-	slender
S	A	10. recto	-	verso
S	A	11. obtain	-	procure
S	A	12. tenuous	-	substantial
S	A	13. impertinent	-	rude
S	A	14. direct	-	roundabout
S	A	15. retinue	-	entourage

2. <u>CORPOR-, CORP(US)-; REG-, (RIG-), RECT-; SIMIL-, SIMUL-; TEMPER- TEMPOR-</u>

Match each word with the best definition.

____ 1. corpus	A. worldly
____ 2. incorporate	B. to disembody
____ 3. regular	C. infectious viral disease of animals
____ 4. erect	D. upright in position
____ 5. insurrection	E. to combine into one body
____ 6. directive	F. customary
____ 7. assemble	G. occurring at the same time
____ 8. simultaneous	H. large collection of writings
____ 9. temporal	I. outburst of anger
____ 10. distemper	J. to bring together
	K. rebellion
	L. an order

3. <u>TEN-, (TIN-), TENT-</u>

Match each word with the best definition.*

____	1. abstention	A.	holding students after school as punishment
____	2. detention	B.	food; nourishment
____	3. entertainment	C.	memory
____	4. maintenance	D.	relevance
____	5. pertinence	E.	a vote neither for nor against
____	6. retention	F.	amusement; hospitality
____	7. sustenance	G.	means of support or subsistence

*The verbs that correspond to these nouns end in -tain: *abstain*, *contain*, etc.

4. Indicate whether each statement is true or false by circling T or F.

T   F   1. The constellation *Aquarius* is the "water carrier."

T   F   2. A *simulcast* is a program broadcast at the same time on radio and TV.

T   F   3. A *contentious* person is congenial and easygoing.

T   F   4. *Bus* is a shortened form of "omnibus."

T   F   5. A *pastor* is the "shepherd" of a spiritual flock, a congregation.

T   F   6. *Aqua vitae* (the water of life) refers to strong liquor.

T   F   7. *Charisma* ultimately derives from the base CANT-.

T   F   8. The prefix ad- has been assimilated in the word *aversion*.

T   F   9. *Attenuate* and *extenuate* are opposite in meaning.

T   F   10. -PLY is the French form of the Latin base PLIC-.

T   F   11. *Resemblance* and *similarity* mean the same thing.

T   F   12. People who *abjure* physical exercise "swear by" (i.e., heartily recommend) it.

T   F   13. The verb *expunge* derives from the Latin ex- + SPONG- + the suffix -e.

T   F   14. A *centurion* is a person celebrating a 100th birthday.

T   F   15. *Leprechaun* ultimately derives from the base CORPOR-, CORP(US)-.

5. Circle the letter of the definition that best fits the underscored word.

1. <u>extenuating</u> circumstances: (A) damning (B) embarrassing (C) providing an excuse

2. resolved to <u>temporize</u>: (A) to postpone a decision (B) to dine on tempura
   (C) to make more even-tempered

3. a Shakespeare <u>omnibus</u>: (A) best seller (B) a book of reprinted works
   (C) a book for ready reference

4. <u>corporal</u> punishment: (A) capital (B) bodily (C) agonizing

5. a <u>tenable</u> thesis: (A) consisting of ten parts (B) unsupportable (C) logical

6. a musical <u>ensemble</u>: (A) group (B) composition (C) interlude

7. Roman <u>aqueducts</u>: (A) conduits for carrying water great distances (B) temples
   (C) water clocks

8. an assembled <u>corps</u>: (A) unclaimed dead bodies (B) a military body
   (C) the complete and unabridged works of an author

9. <u>contemporary</u> poetry: (A) of the present time (B) short-lived (C) abstruse

10. a <u>rector</u>: (A) toy construction set (B) clergyman (C) terminal section of the intestine

6. <u>TEND-, TENT-, TENS-</u>

Match each word with the best definition.*

____ 1. attendance	A. purpose
____ 2. contention	B. the state of being expanded: dilation
____ 3. distention	C. false allegation or justification
____ 4. extension	D. competition; conflict
____ 5. intention	E. the act of being present
____ 6. portent	F. the act of supervising
____ 7. pretense	G. omen
____ 8. superintendence	H. a granting of extra time to complete a project

*The verbs that correspond to these nouns end in -tend: *attend*, *contend*, etc.

7. Words of Interest. Supply the appropriate word from the list below.

1. wide mouthed pitcher _____

2. violent windstorm _____

3. skillful; dexterous _____

4. to meddle in a harmful manner _____

5. funereal hymn _____

6. garment that lends support _____

7. portable cloth shelter _____

8. the trappings or privileges of royalty _____

9. easing of tensions between nations _____

10. emotional characteristics _____

11. a bouquet of flowers worn at the wrist or shoulder _____

12. one who leases a building or property _____

13. clothing; apparel _____

14. embarrassing mishap _____

15. game played with rackets _____

adroit	dirge	temperament
contretemps	dress	tempest
corsage	ewer	tenant
corset	regalia	tennis
détente	tamper	tent

8. Review: Try to supply the appropriate word before referring to the list of possible answers below.

1. Social scientists describe a person who is "turned inward" as an _____ and one is "turned outward" as an _____.

2. A synonym for "to copy," which etymologically means "to fold twice," is _____.

3. A club that is _____ "shuts out" certain people.

4. Extraterrestrials are also called _____ because it is assumed that they will be strange or different from earthlings.

5. A cautious person who "looks all around" before acting is described as _____.

6. Etymologically, an _____ is an exclamatory, obscene word that "fills out" a person's vocabulary.

7. A place where sick or weak people are cared for is called an _____.

8. The adjective _____ applies to sociable persons who like to be part of a "flock" of people.

9. In a court of law, a person who lies under oath is guilty of _____.

10. A problem so "thoroughly folded or tangled" that it is baffling can be described as _____.

11. A synonym for *world*, which etymologically means "a turning as one," is _____.

12. The adjectives *allusive*, *elusive*, and *illusive* are sometimes confused. _____ means "evasive"; _____ means "deceptive"; _____ means "indirectly referred to."

13. The word _____, which etymologically means "foot of a crane," is a synonym for *lineage*.

14. One who is _____ is multi-talented; such a person is "capable of being turned" in many ways.

15. The adjective _____ can refer to someone traveling on foot as well as to something ordinary or commonplace.

aliens	extrovert	pedigree
circumspect	gregarious	perjury
duplicate	infirmary	perplexing
exclusive	introvert	universe
expletive	pedestrian	versatile

LESSON IX

1. Word Analysis. For each word, circle the letter of the correct analysis.

1. biped:
   - (A) two, twice/part
   - (B) good, well/foot
   - (C) good, well/part
   - (D) two, twice/foot

2. introversive:
   - (A) between/to turn
   - (B) between/voice, to call
   - (C) within/to turn
   - (D) within/voice, to call

3. recessive:
   - (A) out, from/to go, to yield
   - (B) out, from/to run, to go
   - (C) back, again/to go, to yield
   - (D) back, again/to run, to go

4. unanimous:
   - (A) one/mind, feeling, life
   - (B) not/year
   - (C) one/year
   - (D) not/mind, feeling, life

5. discursive:
   - (A) to, toward/cure, care
   - (B) to, toward/to run, go
   - (C) in different directions/cure, care
   - (D) in different directions/to run, go

6. devious:
   - (A) down, off/to see
   - (B) down, off/way, road
   - (C) through/to see
   - (D) through/way, road

7. prospective:
   - (A) through/sacred
   - (B) forward, for/to look
   - (C) forward, for/sacred
   - (D) through/to look

8. complementary:
   - (A) against/to fill
   - (B) against/to fold, to tangle
   - (C) with, together/to fold, to tangle
   - (D) with, together/to fill

9. prelusory:
   - (A) before/to play, to mock
   - (B) before/to shut
   - (C) through/to shut
   - (D) through/to play, to mock

10. evidential:
    - (A) forward/way, road
    - (B) forward/to see
    - (C) out, from/way, road
    - (D) out, from/to see

11. circumlocutory:
    - (A) with/to play, to mock
    - (B) around/to play, to mock
    - (C) with/to speak
    - (D) around/to speak

12. superannuated:
    - (A) over, above/year
    - (B) under, below/year
    - (C) over, above/mind, feeling, life
    - (D) under, below/mind, feeling, life

2. Words of Interest. Supply the appropriate word from the list below.

	Word	Etymological Meaning	Current Meaning
1.	_____	clever invention	locomotive; motor
2.	_____	a monastic hood	a game-piece with spots
3.	_____	removal of the dishes	last course of a meal
4.	_____	a stopping place	a public promenade
5.	_____	a breathing upon	divine inspiration
6.	_____	the light-bearer	Satan
7.	_____	flame	a large, wading bird
8.	_____	mastery	a prison
9.	_____	puffed up	a baked dish made of eggs
10.	_____	a house	hemispherical roof
11.	_____	blazing	shocking; notorious
12.	_____	to illuminate manuscripts	to depict
13.	_____	having flame-like curves	highly ornate
14.	_____	side by side	security for a loan
15.	_____	separated	more than a few

afflatus	engine	limn
collateral	flagrant	Lucifer
dessert	flamboyant	parade
dome	flamenco	penitentiary
domino	flamingo	several
dungeon	ingenuity	soufflé

3. <u>DOM(IN)-; FLAG(R)-, FLAM(M)-; LUC-, LUMIN-; PAR-; SEN-; SERV-</u>

Match each word with the best definition.

_____ 1. condominium	A. a large, destructive fire
_____ 2. dominant	B. attire
_____ 3. domain	C. to assist in a minor capacity
_____ 4. domicile	D. self-restrained
_____ 5. conflagration	E. priority gained through length of service
_____ 6. illuminate	F. place of residence
_____ 7. pellucid	G. to deflect; to evade
_____ 8. parry	H. to enlighten
_____ 9. pare	I. to remove by cutting
_____ 10. apparel	J. realm
_____ 11. seniority	K. prevailing
_____ 12. senectitude	L. slavery
_____ 13. subserve	M. old age
_____ 14. reserved	N. a purchased apartment
_____ 15. servitude	O. clear

4. Indicate whether each statement is true or false by circling T or F.

T   F   1. *Flammable* and *inflammable* are opposite in meaning.

T   F   2. Einstein was a *luminary* in the field of physics.

T   F   3. The noun *preserves*, as in "fruit preserves," does not derive from the base SERV-.

T   F   4. Originality and cleverness are characteristic of an *indigenous* idea.

T   F   5. The Latin base PAR- also can mean "equal" and "to give birth."

T   F   6. *Flambeau,* a large ornamental candlestick, does not derive from the Latin base FLAM(M)-.

T   F   7. The word *lunatic* illustrates a once commonly held belief that phases of the moon affect a person's behavior.

T   F   8. The etymology of the Spanish *señor* is "older [person]."

T   F   9. *Danger* ultimately derives from the DOM(IN)- family of words.

T   F   10. The etymological meaning of *lucubration* is close to the expression "burning the midnight oil."

5. <u>GEN-, GENER-; GEN-</u>

Match each word with the best definition.

____	1. congenital	A.	agreeable
____	2. genre	B.	offspring; descendant
____	3. disingenuous	C.	to begin to grow; to sprout
____	4. gender	D.	selfish
____	5. gentle	E.	unselfish
____	6. progeny	F.	mild
____	7. generalize	G.	an artless, innocent young girl
____	8. congenial	H.	existing at birth
____	9. ingénue	I.	classification as to sex
____	10. generous	J.	capable of being produced
____	11. regenerate	K.	category of artistic composition
____	12. generic products	L.	goods sold by type or kind, not by brand name
____	13. genuine	M.	to produce anew
____	14. genetics	N.	to make universal or indefinite
____	15. germinate	O.	the science of heredity
		P.	insincere; calculating
		Q.	authentic

6. Review: The French Connection. The words in this exercise have entered English through French. From the list below, supply the base from which each word derives.

1. align   _____

2. pawn   _____

3. ingredient   _____

4. bonny   _____

5. egalitarian   _____

6. regime   _____

7. damsel   _____

8. enclosure   _____

9. grievous   _____

10. portion   _____

11. convey   _____

12. revenue   _____

13. pansy   _____

14. abound   _____

15. premiere   _____

BENE-, BON-   PED-
CLUD-, CLUS-   PEND-, PENS-
DOM(IN)-   PRIM-
EQU-, (IQU-)   REG-, (RIG-), RECT-
GRAD-, GRESS-   UND-
GRAV-   VEN-, VENT-
LINE-   VI(A)-
PART-

7. Review: Circle the letter of the one word in each group that is <u>not</u> similar in meaning to the other two.

1. (A) vista
   (B) venue
   (C) view

2. (A) comprehension
   (B) recompense
   (C) compensation

3. (A) priority
   (B) precedence
   (C) preview

4. (A) ingenuity
   (B) complicity
   (C) inventiveness

5. (A) pliant
   (B) supple
   (C) suppliant

6. (A) egress
   (B) regress
   (C) degenerate

7. (A) redound
   (B) unite
   (C) combine

8. (A) ponderous
   (B) pendulous
   (C) grave

9. (A) pusillanimous
   (B) magnanimous
   (C) benevolent

10. (A) comply
    (B) transgress
    (C) observe

11. (A) equivocal
    (B) equivalent
    (C) similar

12. (A) spite
    (B) malice
    (C) redoubt

13. (A) deference
    (B) respect
    (C) deferment

14. (A) limn
    (B) temper
    (C) delineate

15. (A) luminous
    (B) flagrant
    (C) perspicuous

16. (A) precede
    (B) prevent
    (C) preclude

17. (A) accede
    (B) assent
    (C) proceed

18. (A) secure
    (B) detain
    (C) fortify

19. (A) improvised
    (B) extemporaneous
    (C) contretemps

20. (A) separate
    (B) habitual
    (C) individual

LESSON X

1. <u>SAL-, (SIL-), SALT-, (SULT-)</u>

Match each word with the best definition.

____	1. insult	A. a fish that leaps
____	2. assail	B. leaping from one topic to the next: random
____	3. resilient	C. fond of jumping: lecherous
____	4. salacious	D. a sudden rush of troops: a rushing [forward]
____	5. salmon	E. the consequence of leaping back
____	6. salient	F. to leap at: attack
____	7. sally (n.)	G. the act of jumping for joy: rejoicing
____	8. exultation	H. to jump on someone: to offend
____	9. desultory	I. capable of leaping back after a mishap
____	10. result	J. striking: [a point] leaping at you

2. Indicate whether each statement is true or false by circling T or F.

T   F   1. The etymological meaning of *terrier* is "earth-dog."

T   F   2. The word *venom* derives from the base VEN-, VENT- (to come).

T   F   3. A *retrospective* view looks to the future.

T   F   4. A *confidant* is a person who can be trusted to keep secrets.

T   F   5. Those suffering from extreme acrophobia are likely to keep their feet on *terra firma*.

T   F   6. The etymology of *candidate* reflects the notion that a person running for political office should be "pure."

T   F   7. The word *compunction* may refer to hesitation in making a decision because of moral issues.

T   F   8. A *coherent* discussion "sticks together" logically.

T   F   9. The etymology of *salad* is "leaping" or "tossed" vegetables.

T   F   10. If something is performed in a *cursory* manner, it is done hastily, as though on the run.

3. Words of Interest. Supply the appropriate word from the list below.

	Word	Etymological Meaning	Current Meaning
1.	_____	power	a small force with legal authority
2.	_____	lacking faith	timid; shy
3.	_____	to lie on	to sit on eggs in order to hatch them
4.	_____	a sitting (by the enemy)	blockade
5.	_____	a leaping over	acrobatic movement in which the body makes a full revolution
6.	_____	a sitting	a meeting of spiritualists
7.	_____	sleeping compartment	carrel
8.	_____	unknown land	exploration of a new field of knowledge
9.	_____	to sit in power	to own; to control
10.	_____	faithful	canine appellation
11.	_____	baked earth	fired clay used for roofing tiles, pottery, etc.
12.	_____	to leap	to cook in a small amount of fat
13.	_____	one promised	man engaged to be married
14.	_____	to put in the earth	to bury a dead body
15.	_____	a beginning	introduction to a discourse

cubicle	incubate	séance
diffident	inter	siege
exordium	posse	somersault
fiancé	possess	terra cotta
financée	Rover	terra incognita
Fido	sauté	territory

4. <u>CUMB-, CUB-; FID-; FIDEL-; HER-, HES-; ORD(IN)-; POT-, POSS-; SED-, (SID-), SESS-; TERR-</u>

Match each word with the best definition.

_____ 1. succumb

_____ 2. covey

_____ 3. concubine

_____ 4. defiant

_____ 5. fiduciary

_____ 6. affiance

_____ 7. adhesive (n.)

_____ 8. hesitant

_____ 9. coordinate

_____ 10. extraordinary

_____ 11. impotent

_____ 12. session

_____ 13. subsidy

_____ 14. supersede

_____ 15. Terre Haute

A. city in Indiana located on high ground

B. exceedingly powerful

C. small group of game birds

D. to yield to a superior force

E. meeting during which a particular activity takes place

F. rebellious

G. to pledge in marriage

H. person to whom property is entrusted for another's benefit

 I. remarkable

J. slow to act

K. a grant of money

L. powerless

M. in some polygamous societies, a second wife

N. glue, for example

O. to supplant

P. bondsman

Q. to place in harmonious relation

5. Indicate the correct answer by circling A or B.

1. obligatory: (A) recumbent   (B) incumbent

2. excessive: (A) inordinate   (B) subordinate

3. capable of becoming: (A) potential   (B) potable

4. to tranquilize: (A) sedate   (B) reside

5. primitive: (A) ordinal   (B) primordial

6. powerfulness: (A) potency   (B) pottage

7. disagreement: (A) dissidence   (B) residence

8. a broad, deep dish: (A) terrene   (B) tureen

9. additional pay given to a performer: (A) residuals   (B) residue

10. allied: (A) confederate   (B) confident

11. diligent: (A) assiduous   (B) insidious

12. intrinsic: (A) incoherent   (B) inherent

13. treachery: (A) fealty   (B) perfidy

14. to make secondary: (A) suborn   (B) subordinate

15. to remove a body from the earth: (A) disinter   (B) deter

6. Review: Supply the missing prefix or base.

1. to enlighten   il _ _ _ _ _ ate

2. bodily   _ _ _ _ _ _ eal

3. powerless   _ _ potent

4. watery   _ _ _ eous

5. to beget   _ _ _ _ _ ate

6. a singing back; retraction   _ _ cantation

7. one fourth   _ _ _ _ _ er

8. earthly   _ _ _ _ estrial

9. kingly   _ _ _ al

10. home   _ _ _ icile

11. combustible   in _ _ _ _ _ able

12. lasting for a short time only   t _ _ _ _ _ ary

7. Review: Indicate the correct answer by circling A or B.

1. native: (A) indigenous   (B) indigent

2. clever: (A) ingenuous   (B) ingenious

3. to communicate: (A) convey   (B) convoy

4. prayerful: (A) precarious   (B) precatory

5. impromptu: (A) contemporary   (B) extempore

6. dead body: (A) corps   (B) corpse

7. forebear: (A) primogenitor   (B) primogeniture

8. tenet: (A) principal   (B) principle

9. natural inclination: (A) preponderance   (B) propensity

10. to move the emotions: (A) affect   (B) effect

11. final dinner course: (A) desert   (B) dessert

12. countenance: (A) visage   (B) visa

13. deliberate self-denial: (A) containment   (B) continence

14. maliciousness: (A) respite   (B) spite

15. to gather together: (A) assemble   (B) assimilate

8. Review: Circle the letter of the correct answer.

1. In the word *abbreviate*, the unassimilated form of the prefix is:
   (A) a-, ab-, abs-   (B) ad-   (C) brev-   (D) -iate

2. Which of the following information about Roman numerals is incorrect?
   (A) V = 5   (B) X = 10   (C) D = 1000   (D) L = 50

3. The Latin base PAR- does <u>not</u> mean:
   (A) to give birth to   (B) equal   (C) abnormal   (D) to make ready

4. Which of the following words is not a hybrid?
   (A) petrify   (B) duplex   (C) gentleman   (D) automobile

5. Which of the following prefixes cannot mean "not"?
   (A) de-   (B) dis-   (C) in-   (D) non-

6. Which one of the following does not apply to prefixes?
   (A) indicates part of speech   (B) negates meaning of base   (C) intensifies meaning of base   (D) indicates direction

7. The month of March owes its name to:
   (A) John Philip Sousa   (B) the Roman god Mars   (C) the Roman numeral five
   (D) the German custom of telling *märchen* or folk tales in spring

8. The term *obsolete* refers to:
   (A) the true meaning of a word   (B) the current meaning of a word   (C) a word or meaning no longer in use   (D) a word or meaning no longer in use except for certain special usages

9. The term *acronym* refers to:
   (A) the removal of a letter at the beginning of a word   (B) words like NATO and MASH
   (C) the removal of a suffix   (D) a word formed from bases of different languages

10. Which of the following had the <u>greatest</u> impact on English:
    (A) Caesar's invasion of Gaul   (B) the conversion of the Angles, Jutes, and Saxons to Christianity   (C) the emperor Claudius' invasion of the British Isles in the 1st century of our era   (D) the Renaissance

LESSON XI

1. Indicate whether the following pairs are synonyms or antonyms by circling S or A.

S	A	1. docile	-		intractable
S	A	2. contiguous	-		adjacent
S	A	3. train	-		retinue
S	A	4. trace	-		hint
S	A	5. fallacious	-		veracious
S	A	6. confess	-		deny
S	A	7. moderate	-		extreme
S	A	8. tangent	-		digression
S	A	9. mutable	-		constant
S	A	10. retreat	-		advance
S	A	11. accredit	-		certify
S	A	12. commute	-		exchange
S	A	13. miscreant	-		infidel
S	A	14. doctrine	-		tenet
S	A	15. contingency	-		certainty

2. <u>TRACT-</u>

Match each word with the best definition.*

____ 1. abstract	A. disparagement
____ 2. attraction	B. written agreement
____ 3. contract	C. recantation
____ 4. detraction	D. charm
____ 5. distraction	E. deduction
____ 6. extraction	F. a lengthening
____ 7. protraction	G. diversion
____ 8. retraction	H. summary
____ 9. subtraction	I. lineage

*The verbs that correspond to these nouns end in -tract: *abstract*, *attract*, *contract*, etc.

3. Words of Interest. Supply the appropriate word from the list below.

1. legendary _____

2. a coward _____

3. contemporary _____

4. foot-soldiery _____

5. to accord as a favor _____

6. essential to the whole _____

7. a fixture for drawing liquids _____

8. moderate estimate of one's abilities _____

9. a contribution of income to support
   a government _____

10. lit. a false step: social blunder _____

11. a low cabinet or cupboard _____

12. a distinguishing feature _____

13. to shed an outer covering _____

14. discernment of the esthetically superior _____

15. failure to fulfill an obligation _____

commode	grant	molt
default	infantry	recreant
fabulous	integral	taste
faucet	modern	tax
faux pas	modesty	trait

4. <u>FA(B)-, FAT-, FAM-</u>

Match each word with the best definition.

____ 1. infamous	A. to speak with: chat
____ 2. fame	B. tale
____ 3. nefarious	C. easy to speak to: pleasant
____ 4. fate	D. what is said about a person: public reputation
____ 5. infant	E. having a bad reputation
____ 6. fatal	F. to take away one's good reputation: malign
____ 7. affable	G. unspeakable: wicked
____ 8. fable	H. pertaining to bad fate: causing death
____ 9. defame	I. that which is said or decreed: destiny
____ 10. confabulate	J. one who cannot speak: baby

5. Indicate whether each statement is true or false by circling T or F.

T   F   1. A *credulous* person tends to be skeptical about the statements of others.

T   F   2. A person who speaks in a *desultory* fashion "leaps" from one topic to the next.

T   F   3. The word *fairy* ultimately derives from the Latin base, FAT-.

T   F   4. A *tactful* person handles situations delicately so as to maintain harmonious relations.

T   F   5. A person who is *tenacious* is persistent; but a person who is *pertinacious* can be extremely persistent, hence stubborn.

T   F   6. The word *rehearse* has an agricultural pedigree.

T   F   7. The etymological meaning of *doctor* is "teacher."

T   F   8. Etymologically, *maintain* means "to keep in hand."

T   F   9. The word *treat* belongs to the TRACT- family of words.

T   F   10. The medical term for a female fatality of an automobile accident is *femme fatale*.

6. Review: The French Connection. The words in this exercise have entered English through French. From the list below, supply the base from which each word derives.

1. deuce   _____

2. gendarme   _____

3. embellish   _____

4. point   _____

5. sewer   _____

6. poise   _____

7. limn   _____

8. séance   _____

9. accredit   _____

10. defiant   _____

11. serf   _____

12. détente   _____

13. ensure   _____

14. employ   _____

15. ounce   _____

AQU(A)-	FID-	PUNG-, PUNCT-
BENE-, BON-	GEN-	SED-, (SID-), SESS-
CANT-, (CENT-)	LUC-, LUMIN-	SERV-
CRED-	PEND-, PENS-	TEND-, TENS- TENT-
CUR-	PLIC-, PLEX-	UN-
DU-	POT-, POSS-	

7. Review: Circle the letter of the one word in each group that is <u>not</u> similar in meaning to the other two.

1. (A) execration
   (B) malignancy
   (C) imprecation

2. (A) unprejudiced
   (B) perspicacious
   (C) impartial

3. (A) digress
   (B) deviate
   (C) deprecate

4. (A) supplication
   (B) complicity
   (C) collusion

5. (A) segregate
   (B) assemble
   (C) convene

6. (A) evoke
   (B) expedite
   (C) educe

7. (A) corpulent
   (B) plenteous
   (C) abundant

8. (A) prelude
   (B) introduction
   (C) counterpoise

9. (A) pertinent
   (B) applicable
   (C) contrary

10. (A) accomplice
    (B) accessory
    (C) malefactor

11. (A) pedestrian
    (B) provident
    (C) prosaic

12. (A) tenet
    (B) dispensation
    (C) doctrine

13. (A) occlude
    (B) expunge
    (C) annihilate

14. (A) intervene
    (B) intercross
    (C) intercede

15. (A) modern
    (B) contemporary
    (C) omnipotent

16. (A) appoint
    (B) proceed
    (C) progress

17. (A) avouch
    (B) affirm
    (C) aggregate

18. (A) apparel
    (B) habiliments
    (C) entreaty

19. (A) retraction
    (B) recantation
    (C) reversion

20. (A) confabulation
    (B) ordinance
    (C) conversation

8. Review: Food. Match each word with the base from which it derives.

____	1. onion	A. BENE-, BON-
____	2. bonbon	B. BI-, BIN-
____	3. dessert	C. CRUC-
____	4. tenderloin	D. FLAG(R)-, FLAM(M)-
____	5. salmon	E. FLAT-
____	6. flambé	F. MOD-
____	7. hot cross bun	G. SAL-, (SIL-), SALT-, (SULT-)
____	8. biscuit	H. SERV-
____	9. soufflé	I. TEND-, TENT-, TENS-
____	10. à la mode	J. UN-

9. Review: Match each word with the best definition.

____	1. seniority	A. general agreement
____	2. reservoir	B. supplies
____	3. countenance	C. priority
____	4. obloquy	D. face
____	5. quintessence	E. to disapprove strongly
____	6. provisions	F. a place where something is saved
____	7. excursus	G. digression
____	8. consensus	H. damage to one's reputation
____	9. closet	I. small room used for storage
____	10. deprecate	J. the fifth and supreme element

LESSON XII

1. Using your knowledge of Latin elements, circle the letter of the correct answer.

1. Trees whose leaves "fall down" annually are called: (A) deciduous (B) defoliants   (C) defunct

2. A star that rapidly grows in brilliance and then fades is called a(n): (A) nova   (B) meteorite   (C) asteroid

3. Which of the following words can mean "reddish"?   (A) fervid (B) fervent   (C) florid

4. Someone who does all kinds of work is called a: (A) malfeasant (B) defeatist   (C) factotum

5. What medical practice attempts to cure illness by "puncturing with a needle"? (A) biofeedback   (B) vivisection   (C) acupuncture

6. "The Occident" is another name for the: (A) West   (B) South   (C) East

7. All of the following words have to do with "sharpness." Which one refers to mental keenness?   (A) acumen   (B) acrimony   (C) acidity

8. Something that "flows like honey" (a sweet-sounding voice, for example) is said to be: (A) mellivorous   (B) mellifluous   (C) melliferous

9. Someone who is "flowing" with wealth is said to be: (A) magnanimous (B) affluent   (C) munificent

10. A disease once thought to be caused by the "influence" of the heavenly bodies is called: (A) bubonic plague   (B) influenza   (C) malaria

11. A person whose speech "flows readily," especially in a foreign language, is said to be: (A) logorrheic   (B) fluent   (C) eloquent

12. Small bits of colored paper thrown at ticker-tape parades are called: (A) confetti   (B) comfits   (C) confections

13. The heading of an article or document that catches a person's attention is called a: (A) caitiff   (B) caption   (C) cable

14. Which state is named after the Feast of Flowers?   (A) California (B) Nevada   (C) Florida

2. <u>CAP-, (CIP-), CAPT-, (CEPT-)</u>

Match each word with the best definition.

____ 1. anticipate		A. idea; notion
____ 2. emancipate		B. seizure and control of an area
____ 3. concept		C. container
____ 4. inception		D. to free
____ 5. intercept		E. spacious
____ 6. receptacle		F. easily influenced by something
____ 7. deception		G. a beginning
____ 8. capacious		H. fraud
____ 9. occupation		I. to cut off from a destination
____ 10. susceptible		J. to expect; to foresee

3. <u>FAC-, (FIC-), FACT-, (FECT-)</u>

Match each word with the best definition.

____ 1. satisfaction		A. contagious
____ 2. proficiency		B. to wipe out; to destroy
____ 3. feature (v.)		C. easy; glib
____ 4. affectation		D. an aspect or phase
____ 5. deficit		E. pretension; airs
____ 6. interface		F. seditious
____ 7. efface		G. skill; ability
____ 8. superficial		H. to make better
____ 9. factious		I. to suppress
____ 10. feasible		J. gratification
____ 11. facet		K. confusion; embarrassment
____ 12. facile		L. to give prominence to
____ 13. discomfiture		M. capable of being done
____ 14. counterfeit		N. shortage
____ 15. infectious		O. shallow
		P. forgery
		Q. program designed to communicate information from one computer to another

4. Circle the letter of the one word in each group that is <u>not</u> similar in meaning to the other two.

1. (A) affluent
   (B) facilitative
   (C) abundant

2. (A) defect
   (B) efficacy
   (C) fault

3. (A) exacerbate
   (B) aggravate
   (C) evoke

4. (A) incidence
   (B) incumbency
   (C) occurrence

5. (A) redundant
   (B) superfluous
   (C) superannuated

6. (A) adroit
   (B) acrid
   (C) pungent

7. (A) feat
   (B) regimen
   (C) exploit

8. (A) corpse
   (B) cadaver
   (C) corps

9. (A) provenance
   (B) preconception
   (C) prejudice

10. (A) infectious
    (B) contagious
    (C) redintegrative

11. (A) facsimile
    (B) facetiousness
    (C) replica

12. (A) factitious
    (B) artificial
    (C) factious

13. (A) fatal
    (B) internecine
    (C) efficacious

14. (A) captivate
    (B) charm
    (C) besiege

15. (A) incorrigible
    (B) incredible
    (C) inconceivable

16. (A) temporarily
    (B) coincidently
    (C) simultaneously

17. (A) fallacious
    (B) deceptive
    (C) ineffable

18. (A) occasion
    (B) concurrence
    (C) event

19. (A) decadence
    (B) degeneration
    (C) delineation

20. (A) munificence
    (B) generosity
    (C) avoirdupois

21. (A) innocent
    (B) culpable
    (C) ingenuous

22. (A) salacious
    (B) flagrant
    (C) infamous

5. Words of Interest. Supply the appropriate word from the list below.

1. the principal house of a landed estate   _____

2. a type of peach   _____

3. to defraud   _____

4. female member of a royal family   _____

5. object believed to have magical power   _____

6. a portable case for carrying loose
   sheets of paper   _____

7. a fever marked by chills   _____

8. an umbrella-like device that opens midair
   and guards against a fall   _____

9. "sour wine"   _____

10. ground meal of a grain   _____

11. set of instructions for making a food dish   _____

12. uncorrupted by evil   _____

13. to regain health   _____

14. to provide food for a large party   _____

15. impatiently expectant   _____

ague	flour	portfolio
cater	hacienda	princess
cheat	innocent	recipe
eager	nectarine*	recover
fetish	parachute	vinegar

*Related to the NEC-, NIC- base.

6. Supply the missing base.

1. to make new again   re _ _ _ ate

2. harmless   in _ _ _ uous

3. leafage   _ _ _ _ age

4. waterfall   _ _ _ cade

5. harmful   _ _ _ ious

6. a place where things are made   _ _ _ _ ory

7. keenness of perception   _ _ _ men

8. continued flow   f _ _ _

9. bearing flowers   _ _ _ _ iferous

10. to take prisoner   _ _ _ _ ure

7. Review: Indicate whether the following pairs are synonyms or antonyms by circling S or A.

S	A	1. preface	-	exordium
S	A	2. impedimenta	-	obstacles
S	A	3. accidental	-	adventitious
S	A	4. deceit	-	duplicity
S	A	5. profit	-	benefit
S	A	6. superfluity	-	excess
S	A	7. defame	-	malign
S	A	8. dubious	-	certain
S	A	9. florid	-	ornate
S	A	10. integrity	-	completeness
S	A	11. fashion	-	mold
S	A	12. salient	-	inconspicuous
S	A	13. tact	-	diplomacy
S	A	14. sedate	-	impassioned
S	A	15. casual	-	formal

8. Review: Supply the missing letters to form an Anglo-Saxon equivalent of each Latinate word.

1. domicile   h _ _ _

2. genus   k _ _ _

3. credible   b _ _ _ _ _ able

4. terrestrial   e _ _ _ _ ly

5. illuminate   en _ _ _ _ _ en

6. similar   l _ _ _

7. sentiment   f _ _ _ ing

8. vision   s _ _ _ _

9. incorporate   em _ _ _ _

10. fable   t _ _ _

9. Review: Complete each statement by supplying the meaning of the base.

1. The base in *peon, pioneer*, and *pedestal*   means _____.

2. The base in *clairvoyant, vista,* and *video*   means _____.

3. The base in *sire, senator,* and *senescence*   means _____.

4. The base in *effort, fortress,* and *comforting*   means _____.

5. The base in *travesty, vest,* and *divest*   means _____.

6. The base in *assault, insult,* and *salience*   means _____.

7. The base in *dime, decimate,* and *December*   means _____.

8. The base in *session, sediment,* and *séance*   means _____.

9. The base in *crucial, crux,* and *cruise*   means _____.

10. The base in *cede, deceased,* and *success*   means _____.

11. The base in *tendon, tent,* and *tense*   means _____.

12. The base in *ludicrous, illusionist,* and *prelude*   means _____.

13. The base in *convene, venue,* and *invent*   means _____.

14. The base in *elucidate, pellucid,* and *Lucy*   means _____.

15. The base in *vertebra, versatile,* and *divorce*   means _____.

LESSON XIII

1. FUS-

Match each word with the best definition.*

____ 1. confuse   A. to inspire; to introduce

____ 2. defuse   B. to overspread with liquid, color, etc.

____ 3. effuse   C. to deny

____ 4. infuse   D. to perplex; to confound

____ 5. interfuse   E. to pour out; to exude

____ 6. refuse   F. to intermingle; to blend one with another

____ 7. suffuse   G. to transfer from one source to another

____ 8. transfuse   H. to deprive of intent to harm

*The nouns that correspond to these verbs end in -fusion: *confusion*, *effusion*, etc. (The verb *defuse* lacks a noun counterpart.)

2. Indicate whether the following pairs are synonyms or antonyms by circling S or A.

S	A	1. native	-	foreign
S	A	2. decomposition	-	decay
S	A	3. tortuous	-	winding
S	A	4. apposite	-	relevant
S	A	5. dispel	-	assemble
S	A	6. refuse	-	trash
S	A	7. torment	-	suffering
S	A	8. extortionate	-	reasonable
S	A	9. pregnant	-	meaningful
S	A	10. postpone	-	defer
S	A	11. opponent	-	ally
S	A	12. expound	-	explain
S	A	13. duress	-	coercion
S	A	14. distort	-	misrepresent
S	A	15. appealing	-	repulsive

3. Words of Interest. Supply the appropriate word from the list below.

Word	Etymological Meaning	Current Meaning
1. _____	hard	sullen; gloomy
2. _____	something twisted	a portable light
3. _____	rebirth	period of revival of humanistic learning
4. _____	secret-keeper	clerical worker
5. _____	a twisted chain	twisted metal collar worn by ancient Gauls and Britons
6. _____	born later; younger	weak; insignificant
7. _____	accusation	unlawful activity
8. _____	nose-twister	a plant with pungent leaves and seeds
9. _____	pouring easily	ineffectual; useless
10. _____	agreement	public performance of music
11. _____	a setting down or aside	railroad or bus station
12. _____	decision	an order having the force of law
13. _____	natural	unsophisticated
14. _____	something twisted back	witty reply

concert	futile	Renaissance
crime	naïve	retort
decree	nasturtium	secretary
depot	peal	torch
dour	puny	torque

4. -POSE

Match each word with the best definition.

____	1. compose	A. to obtrude upon
____	2. depose	B. to put forward: to offer
____	3. expose	C. to conjecture
____	4. impose	D. to put down: to overthrow
____	5. juxtapose	E. to lay open to view
____	6. oppose	F. to create; to fashion
____	7. propose	G. to place over or above something else
____	8. repose	H. to lie at rest
____	9. superimpose	I. to set against: to resist
____	10. suppose	J. to place beside, for comparison or contrast

5. PEL(L)-, PULS-

Supply the missing prefix.*

1. to drive forward   ____ pel

2. to drive out   ____ pel

3. to drive back   ____ pel

4. to drive on or against   ____ pel

5. to drive together forcibly ____ pel

*The nouns that correspond to these verbs end in -pulsion or -pulse: *compulsion, impulsion, impulse,* etc.; adjectives generally end in -pulsive: *compulsive, impulsive,* etc.

6. Identify the prefix (if any), base, and suffix in each word and then give the meaning of each element.

MEANINGS

   1. con | ting | ent   *with*   *touch*   *-ing* _____

   2. adventitious _____

   3. retentive _____

   4. prelusory _____

   5. immutable _____

   6. adherent _____

   7. docile _____

   8. credulous _____

   9. inordinate _____

 10. infantile _____

 11. vociferant _____

 12. leonine _____

 13. accurate _____

 14. turbid _____

 15. pertinacious _____

7. <u>CERN-, CRET-, [CERT-]</u>

Match each word with the best definition.

____	1. ascertain	A.	prudence
____	2. certain	B.	to throw into confusion
____	3. certificate	C.	to determine
____	4. concern	D.	jumbled
____	5. disconcert	E.	countercharge
____	6. discretion	F.	anxiety; manufacturing company
____	7. excrete	G.	something hidden
____	8. indiscriminate	H.	a diploma, for example
____	9. recrimination	I.	sure
____	10. secret	J.	to eliminate from the body

8. Review: Supply the missing prefix or base.

1. unmistakable	in _ _ _ _ ible
2. tale	_ _ ble
3. manner	_ _ _ e
4. touchable	_ _ _ _ ible
5. foreword	_ _ _ face
6. a genetic change	_ _ _ ation
7. new	_ _ _ el
8. slavery	_ _ _ _ itude
9. birth	_ _ _ ivity
10. word-for-word	_ _ _ _ atim
11. unbelievable	_ _ credible
12. conduit for water	aque _ _ _ _

9. Review: The French Connection. The words in this exercise have entered English through French. From the list below, supply the base from which each word derives.

1. push   _____

2. genteel   _____

3. fealty   _____

4. ordain   _____

5. assess   _____

6. puissance   _____

7. assault   _____

8. grant   _____

9. catch   _____

10. fault   _____

11. retreat   _____

12. nee   _____

13. eager   _____

14. flourish   _____

15. domain   _____

AC(U)-, ACR-, ACET-	NASC-, NAT-
CAP-, (CIP-), CAPT-, (CEPT-)	ORD(IN)-
CRED-	PEL(L)-, PULS-
DOM(IN)-	POT-, POSS-
FALL-, FALS-	SAL-, (SIL-), SALT-, (SULT-)
FIDEL-	SED-, (SID-), SESS-
FLOR-	TRACT-
GEN-	

LESSON XIV

1. The following words have undergone degeneration of meaning. Give both their original and current meanings.

	ORIGINAL MEANING	CURRENT MEANING
1. boor	_____	_____
2. counterfeit	_____	_____
3. disease	_____	_____
4. egregious	_____	_____
5. officious	_____	_____
6. sanctimony	_____	_____
7. silly	_____	_____
8. villain	_____	_____

The following words have undergone elevation of meaning. Give both their original and current meanings.

9. count (=nobleman)	_____	_____
10. engineer	_____	_____
11. frank	_____	_____
12. naughty	_____	_____
13. nice	_____	_____
14. pioneer	_____	_____
15. prestigious	_____	_____
16. urbane	_____	_____

2. <u>AM-; DE-, DIV-; [JOURN-]; OR-; PROB-, [PROV-]; RAP-, RAPT-, (REPT-); STRING-, STRICT-, [STRAIN-]; VER-</u>

Match each word with the best definition.

____ 1. amicable	A.	to suspend until another time
____ 2. amorous	B.	to affirm
____ 3. deify	C.	swift
____ 4. divination	D.	condemnation
____ 5. adjourn	E.	exacting
____ 6. adore	F.	the power of a god: prophecy
____ 7. inexorable	G.	grasping
____ 8. reprove	H.	appearance of the truth
____ 9. probity	I.	to scold
____ 10. disapprobation	J.	to make into a god
____ 11. rapacious	K.	full of love
____ 12. rapid	L.	inquiry
____ 13. surreptitious	M.	integrity; rectitude
____ 14. restrain	N.	performed secretly
____ 15. strict	O.	unyielding
____ 16. verisimilitude	P.	to hold back; to check
____ 17. aver	Q.	to demonstrate again
	R.	friendly
	S.	to revere

3. Words of Interest. Supply the appropriate word from the list below.

1. female lead in an opera   _____

2. anguish of mind or body   _____

3. scoundrel   _____

4. to transport with delight   _____

5. nonprofessional   _____

6. shrine consecrated to a prophetic god   _____

7. day-to-day record of personal experiences   _____

8. judgment; decision   _____

9. to reside temporarily   _____

10. Chinese idol   _____

11. gloomy   _____

12. a fudge confection "next to heaven"   _____

13. farewell   _____

14. influential status   _____

15. "with a round mouth": rich in   _____
    sound; bombastic

adieu	divinity	orotund
amateur	enrapture	prestige
dismal	joss	reprobate
distress	journal	sojourn
diva	oracle	verdict

4. Review: Circle the letter of the one word in each group that is <u>not</u> similar in meaning to the other two.

1. (A) bona fide
   (B) genuine
   (C) pretentious

2. (A) discretion
   (B) confabulation
   (C) circumspection

3. (A) insidious
   (B) fabulous
   (C) magnificent

4. (A) defer
   (B) adjudicate
   (C) postpone

5. (A) excruciate
   (B) torture
   (C) defame

6. (A) tractable
   (B) docile
   (C) dilatory

7. (A) counterpoise
   (B) discompose
   (C) perturb

8. (A) certify
   (B) confirm
   (C) probe

9. (A) congenial
   (B) punctilious
   (C) affable

10. (A) conductor
    (B) accomplice
    (C) confederate

11. (A) intervene
    (B) imprecate
    (C) interpose

12. (A) tenable
    (B) tenacious
    (C) adhesive

13. (A) distort
    (B) pervert
    (C) pertain

14. (A) naïve
    (B) innocent
    (C) disingenuous

15. (A) component
    (B) ingredient
    (C) tort

16. (A) confuse
    (B) replenish
    (C) perplex

17. (A) discernment
    (B) continence
    (C) perception

18. (A) relevant
    (B) intrusive
    (C) apposite

19. (A) incentive
    (B) inducement
    (C) eloquence

20. (A) dominant
    (B) preponderant
    (C) obdurate

REVIEW OF LESSONS VIII–XIV (SELF-TESTING: Answers can be found in Appendix C.)

1. Indicate whether each statement is true or false by circling T or F.

T   F   1. *Repair* (to remedy) and *repair* (to frequent) both derive from the base PATRI-.

T   F   2. *Omnium-gatherum* is a synonym for hodgepodge.

T   F   3. *Corps* is a literary term referring to a body of poetry.

T   F   4. *Nice* has undergone degeneration of meaning.

T   F   5. A *compulsive* person has irresistible urges to do certain things.

T   F   6. The word *fame* originally referred to any report.

T   F   7. Words associated with the country often undergo elevation of meaning.

T   F   8. The word *disease* once referred to any discomfort.

T   F   9. The word *string* ultimately derives from the Latin base STRING-.

T   F   10. Generalization and specialization are types of semantic change.

T   F   11. Originally, *plausible* meant "worthy of applause."

T   F   12. *Sir, senior*, and *monsieur* all derive from the base SEN-.

T   F   13. *Prestige* (originally "juggler's tricks") has undergone elevation of meaning.

T   F   14. Being able to recognize the Latin elements in an English word is an infallible way to determine its current meaning.

T   F   15. *Found* (to establish) and *found* (to melt metal) derive from the same Latin base.

2. Match each suffix with its meaning.

_____ 1. -ity   A. full of

_____ 2. -ble   B. = ing

_____ 3. -ary   C. state of; quality of

_____ 4. -ose   D. one connected with

_____ 5. -ant, -ent, (-ient)   E. able to be; tending to

3. Indicate whether the following pairs are synonyms or antonyms by circling S or A.

S	A	1. enamor	-	captivate
S	A	2. journal	-	diary
S	A	3. composed	-	self-possessed
S	A	4. affluent	-	impecunious
S	A	5. adherent	-	renegade
S	A	6. detain	-	advance
S	A	7. result	-	consequence
S	A	8. acrimony	-	bitterness
S	A	9. adroit	-	dexterous
S	A	10. flammable	-	inflammable
S	A	11. reprove	-	censure
S	A	12. torch	-	flambeau
S	A	13. confident	-	sanguine
S	A	14. servile	-	regal
S	A	15. recumbency	-	repose

4. Occupations. Match each word with the base from which it derives.

____ 1. rector	A. CAD-, (CID-), CAS-
____ 2. servant	B. CERN-, CRET-
____ 3. plenipotentiary	C. CRED-
____ 4. president	D. DOC-, DOCT-
____ 5. doctor	E. DOM(IN)-
____ 6. postmistress	F. FAC-, (FIC-), FACT-, (FECT-)
____ 7. manufacturer	G. FLOR-
____ 8. parachutist	H. GEN-
____ 9. florist	I. ORD(IN)-
____ 10. secretary	J. PON-, POSIT-
____ 11. entertainer	K. POT-, POSS-
____ 12. orderly	L. REG-, (RIG-), RECT-
____ 13. domestic	M. SED-, (SID-), SESS-
____ 14. engineer	N. SERV-
____ 15. creditor	O. TEN-, (TIN-), TENT-

5. Supply the missing base.

1. newborn   neo _ _ _ e

2. person taken (prisoner)   _ _ _ _ ive

3. god-like   _ _ _ ine

4. newness   _ _ _ elty

5. tending to believe   _ _ _ _ ulous

6. truthful   _ _ _ acious

7. speech   _ _ ation

8. having equal sides   equi _ _ _ _ _ al

9. enlightenment   il _ _ _ _ _ ation

10. unchangeable   im _ _ _ able

11. to throb   _ _ _ _ ate

12. place   p _ _ _ _ ion

13. full of love   _ _ orous

14. unlike   dis _ _ _ _ _ ar

15. foreword   pre _ _ ce

16. to embody   in _ _ _ _ _ _ ate

17. to blow into   in _ _ _ _ e

18. full of leaves   _ _ _ _ ose

19. long-lasting   _ _ _ able

20. indeed   in f _ _ _ (two words)

6. Match each word with the best definition.

_____ 1. terrace	A. mutually ruinous
_____ 2. casualty	B. to bear; to suffer patiently
_____ 3. retract	C. temperate
_____ 4. endure	D. accompanying
_____ 5. confederacy	E. patio
_____ 6. degenerate	F. slight
_____ 7. moderate	G. treachery
_____ 8. tenuous	H. to recant
_____ 9. aqua	I. to deteriorate
_____ 10. fallacious	J. machinery
_____ 11. apparatus	K. disagreeable; offensive
_____ 12. attendant	L. person killed or missing in action
_____ 13. obnoxious	M. alliance
_____ 14. perfidy	N. false
_____ 15. internecine	O. light greenish blue

LESSON XV

1. CID-, CIS-; MATR-, MATERN-; PATRI-; SEQU-, SECUT-; SOL-; VIV-

Match each word with the best definition.

____ 1. excise	A. seclusion
____ 2. concise	B. to cut out
____ 3. incision	C. succeeding
____ 4. matriculate	D. succinct
____ 5. expatriate	E. to harass
____ 6. persecute	F. to banish from one's country
____ 7. prosecute	G. to bring back to life
____ 8. subsequent	H. the act of cutting into
____ 9. consequential	I. lifelike
____ 10. solitude	J. to enroll in college
____ 11. vivid	K. to institute legal proceedings
____ 12. revive	L. significant

2. CID-

Match each word with the best definition.

____ 1. fratricide	A. baby-killer
____ 2. genocide	B. brother-killer
____ 3. homicide	C. sister-killer
____ 4. infanticide	D. father- or mother-killer
____ 5. insecticide	E. wife-killer
____ 6. parricide	F. insect eradicator
____ 7. regicide	G. self-killer
____ 8. sororicide	H. killer of another human being
____ 9. suicide	I. king-killer
____ 10. uxoricide	J. extermination of an entire racial or national group

3. Words of Interest. Supply the appropriate word from the list below.

	Word	Etymological Meaning	Current Meaning
1.	_____	it does not follow	illogical inference
2.	_____	stone cuttings	anything that binds or unites
3.	_____	rapid recital of Pater Nosters	a comedian's rapid speech
4.	_____	to father (a deed)	to commit a crime
5.	_____	an exact cut	summary
6.	_____	a person who follows	a man courting a woman
7.	_____	alone	gloomy; sulky
8.	_____	member of the original Roman aristocracy	any person of noble or high rank
9.	_____	pertaining to a banquet	sociable
10.	_____	little cutting tool	tool used to cut stone
11.	_____	fetus cut from the womb	a male monarch
12.	_____	a speaking alone	dramatic monologue
13.	_____	father	form of address to a priest
14.	_____	lonely	bereft of friends
15.	_____	to outlive	to persevere despite hardships

cement	non sequitur	précis
chisel	padre	soliloquy
convivial	patrician	suitor
czar	patter	sullen
desolate	perpetrate	survive

4. <u>MATR-, MATERN-; PATR-, PATERN-; PATRI-; PATRON-</u>

Substitute the base MATR-, MATERN- for PATR-, PATERN-; PATRI-; PATRON-
to form the feminine equivalent of each of the following words. Then give the
meanings of both. (Each pair is not necessarily parallel in meaning.)

MEANING

1. patrilineal

_____

2. patriarch

_____

3. patronymic

_____

4. paternal

_____

5. paternity

_____

6. patricide

_____

7. patrimony

_____

8. patron

_____

5. Indicate whether each statement is true or false by circling T or F.

T   F   1. *Solitaire*, a card game, and *solitaire*, a gem set alone, both derive from the base SOL-, meaning "alone."

T   F   2. *Pattern* derives from the Latin base PATRON-.

T   F   3. A person who kills a parrot is guilty of *parricide*.

T   F   4. In the expression, "it's a beauty," the word *beauty* has shifted from a concrete to an abstract meaning.

T   F   5. A *sequel* continues the narrative of a previous film or literary work.

T   F   6. *Cadaver* belongs to the CID-, CIS- family of words.

T   F   7. The word *hussy* was once simply a variant of "housewife."

T   F   8. The etymological meaning of *assassin* is "eater of corned beef hash."

T   F   9. The noun *suite*, as in "hotel suite," derives from the base SEQU-, SECUT-.

T   F   10. *Courtesan* has undergone degeneration of meaning; the word originally referred to a lady of the court.

6. Review: Circle the letter of the word that best fits the definition.

1. slanderous:
   (A) affable
   (B) ineffable
   (C) defamatory
   (D) nefarious

2. to divert:
   (A) abstract
   (B) distract
   (C) extract
   (D) subtract

3. power:
   (A) affluence
   (B) confluence
   (C) effluence
   (D) influence

4. to betray:
   (A) conceive
   (B) deceive
   (C) perceive
   (D) receive

5. to expand:
   (A) attend
   (B) contend
   (C) distend
   (D) portend

6. to contaminate:
   (A) affect
   (B) effect
   (C) infect
   (D) perfect

7. occurrence:
   (A) cadence
   (B) coincidence
   (C) decadence
   (D) incidence

8. ugly: (A) compulsive   (C) propulsive
                                    (B) expulsive   (D) repulsive

9. to place near: (A) appose   (C) depose
                                    (B) compose   (D) expose

10. a witty reply: (A) distortion   (C) retort
                                    (B) extortion   (D) tort

11. to confine: (A) compound   (C) impound
                                    (B) expound   (D) propound

12. to lie at rest: (A) juxtapose   (C) propose
                                    (B) oppose   (D) repose

13. recovery: (A) anticipation   (C) participation
                                    (B) occupation   (D) recuperation

14. to wield: (A) apply   (C) ply
                                    (B) imply   (D) reply

15. to agree: (A) concur   (C) occur
                                    (B) incur   (D) recur

16. to reveal: (A) close   (C) enclose
                                  (B) disclose   (D) foreclose

17. to accomplish: (A) complement (C) implement
                                  (B) compliment   (D) supplement

18. entreaty: (A) complication (C) implication
                                  (B) explication   (D) supplication

19. to esteem: (A) expect   (C) respect
                                  (B) inspect   (D) suspect

20. candy: (A) affection   (C) infection
                                  (B) confection   (D) refection

21. to bewilder: (A) confuse   (C) infuse
                                  (B) diffuse   (D) perfuse

22. to scold: (A) approve   (C) prove
                                  (B) disprove   (D) reprove

7. Review: The French Connection. The words in this exercise have entered English through French. Match each word with the base from which it derives.

____	1. nuisance	A. AC(U)-, ACR-, ACET-
____	2. succor	B. CED-, CESS-
____	3. grandeur	C. CLUD-,CLUS-
____	4. voice	D. CUR(R)-, CURS-
____	5. relieve	E. FID-
____	6. enclosure	F. GEN-
____	7. detain	G. GRAND-
____	8. repair	H. LEV-
____	9. cease	I. PATRI-
____	10. revenue	J. PREC-
____	11. faith	K. NOC-, NOX-, NIC-, NEC-
____	12. royal	L. REG-, (RIG-), RECT-
____	13. gentry	M. TEN-, (TIN-), TENT-
____	14. ague	N. VEN-, VENT-
____	15. prayer	O. VOC-, VOK-

8. Review: Match each word with its <u>etymological</u> meaning.

____	1. gradual	A. to sit in power
____	2. punctuate	B. power, sovereignty
____	3. possess	C. military group made up of young men
____	4. insult	D. a holy place
____	5. funnel	E. to mark off with dots
____	6. diva	F. take a little of this and a little of that
____	7. genie	G. by steps
____	8. probable	H. a list of words
____	9. danger	I. to leap on
____	10. infantry	J. hard
____	11. tax	K. likely to prove true
____	12. recipe	L. goddess
____	13. dour	M. guardian spirit
____	14. sanctuary	N. little object for pouring
____	15. vocabulary	O. a government's touching of the pocketbook

LESSON XVI

1. Indicate whether the following pairs are synonyms or antonyms by circling S or A.

S	A	1. concrete	-	actual
S	A	2. adjunct	-	assistant
S	A	3. legible	-	readable
S	A	4. negligible	-	significant
S	A	5. dissolute	-	debauched
S	A	6. initiate	-	instruct
S	A	7. elegance	-	grace
S	A	8. summon	-	dismiss
S	A	9. accrue	-	decrease
S	A	10. solution	-	explanation

2. I-, IT-

Match each word with the best definition.

____	1. ambiance	A. route of a journey
____	2. circuitous	B. short-lived
____	3. transitory	C. roundabout; indirect
____	4. exit	D. notice of a person's death
____	5. county	E. atmosphere
____	6. initial	F. to die
____	7. itinerary	G. first letter of a name
____	8. issue	H. a point of a discussion
____	9. obituary	I. the act of going out
____	10. perish	J. originally, territory of a count

3. Circle the letter of the word that best fits the definition.

1. discriminating: (A) collective   (B) elective   (C) selective

2. to command: (A) adjoin   (B) disjoin   (C) enjoin

3. determined: (A) absolute   (B) dissolute   (C) resolute

4. able to pay debts: (A) insolvent   (B) soluble   (C) solvent

5. abnormal growth: (A) crescendo   (B) excrescence (C) increase

6. to conquer: (A) conjoin   (B) conjugate   (C) subjugate

7. to caution: (A) demonstrate (B) admonish   (C) remonstrate

8. bias: (A) predilection (B) recollection (C) selection

9. connecting word: (A) conjunction (B) injunction   (C) junction

10. wandering: (A) itinerant   (B) obituary   (C) perishable

11. answer in reply: (A) adjunctive   (B) injunction   (C) rejoinder

12. beginning step: (A) initiative   (B) issue   (C) transit

13. person who warns: (A) monitor   (B) monstrosity   (C) monument

14. accompanying: (A) concomitant (B) conjugal   (C) conjunctive

15. worthy of selection: (A) electoral   (B) eligible   (C) intellectual

4. Words of Interest. Supply the appropriate word from the list below.

Word	Etymological Meaning	Current Meaning
1. _____	new growth	newly enlisted soldier
2. _____	something to be read	myth
3. _____	companion	European nobleman
4. _____	a warning	hideous creature
5. _____	chosen body of soldiers	Roman military unit
6. _____	council	faction that controls a government after a revolution
7. _____	reminder of great deeds	memorial
8. _____	[military] increase	all personnel manning a ship

9. _____ chosen people   select group

10. _____ a collectible [plant]   a pod used as food

11. _____ pertaining to "getting hitched"   marital

12. _____ a gathering together   series of connected spirals

13. _____ a going around for votes   desire for fame, rank, or power

14. _____ the act of going apart from established authority   rebellion

15. _____ coming up secretly   unforeseen; quick

ambition	cull	monster
coil	elite	monument
conjugal	junta	muster
connubial	legend	recruit
count	legion	sedition
crew	legume	sudden

5. **Review:** The words in this exercise have entered English through Spanish. Match each word with the base from which it derives.

_____ 1. adios   A. AM-

_____ 2. hacienda   B. DE-, DIV-

_____ 3. amigo   C. DOM(IN)-

_____ 4. padre   D. FAC-, (FIC-), FACT-, (FECT-)

_____ 5. don   E. FLAG(R)-, FLAM(M)-

_____ 6. flamingo   F. JUG-, JUNCT-

_____ 7. señorita   G. PATR-, PATERN-

_____ 8. junta   H. SEN-

6. Review: Circle the letter of the one word in each group that is <u>not</u> similar in meaning to the other three.

1. (A) subservient
   (B) obsequious
   (C) unimpeded
   (D) servile

2. (A) intercede
   (B) intervene
   (C) interface
   (D) interpose

3. (A) delineate
   (B) divert
   (C) portray
   (D) limn

4. (A) adherence
   (B) fidelity
   (C) fealty
   (D) feasibility

5. (A) accept
   (B) countenance
   (C) assess
   (D) approve

6. (A) tangent
   (B) digression
   (C) discrimination
   (D) excursion

7. (A) confound
   (B) supersede
   (C) perplex
   (D) confuse

8. (A) defame
   (B) malign
   (C) prepossess
   (D) traduce

9. (A) parent
   (B) progenitor
   (C) progeny
   (D) ancestor

10. (A) tenet
    (B) principle
    (C) doctrine
    (D) recidivism

11. (A) credulous
    (B) veritable
    (C) genuine
    (D) bona fide

12. (A) features
    (B) lineaments
    (C) traits
    (D) perspectives

13. (A) decomposition
    (B) disaffection
    (C) decay
    (D) disintegration

14. (A) assembly
    (B) muster
    (C) collection
    (D) contrast

15. (A) prelusive
    (B) protrusive
    (C) introductory
    (D) prefatory

16. (A) expose
    (B) verify
    (C) jeopardize
    (D) endanger

LESSON XVII

1. FERV-; FRANG-, (FRING-), FRACT-; GRAN-; MINOR-, MINUS-, MINUT-; QUIR-, QUISIT-, QUEST-; SEC-, SEG-, SECT-

Match each word with the best definition.

____ 1. fervency	A. something obligatory
____ 2. defray	B. a natural division
____ 3. refrain (n.)	C. to cut into small pieces
____ 4. refract	D. to "break back" light
____ 5. granite	E. to question
____ 6. granulated	F. investigation
____ 7. minutiae	G. a written order for something
____ 8. mince	H. to be nauseated
____ 9. acquisition	I. trifling details
____ 10. requisition	J. enthusiasm; zeal
____ 11. query (v.)	K. a recurring phrase or verse
____ 12. inquisition	L. a grainy, igneous rock
____ 13. requirement	M. formed into grains
____ 14. vivisection	N. dissection of a live animal
____ 15. segment	O. to pay
	P. something gained
	Q. curiosity

2. Consult a dictionary (if necessary) in order to determine the etymological and current meanings of each of the following diminutives.

	ETYMOLOGICAL	CURRENT
1. armadillo	_____	_____
2. chapel	_____	_____
3. floret	_____	_____
4. gladiolus	_____	_____
5. muscle	_____	_____
6. punctilio	_____	_____

7. pupil   _____   _____

8. receptacle   _____   _____

9. scruple   _____   _____

10. umbrella   _____   _____

3. Indicate whether the following pairs are synonyms or antonyms by circling S or A.

S	A	1. fervor	-	passion
S	A	2. infringe	-	encroach
S	A	3. administer	-	execute
S	A	4. diminutive	-	immense
S	A	5. fragile	-	sturdy
S	A	6. inquisitive	-	curious
S	A	7. fractious	-	quarrelsome
S	A	8. diminish	-	increase
S	A	9. fragmentary	-	whole
S	A	10. garner	-	accumulate
S	A	11. dissect	-	analyze
S	A	12. require	-	forgo
S	A	13. questionnaire	-	survey
S	A	14. ingrain	-	infuse
S	A	15. frailty	-	susceptibility

4. Supply the missing base.

1. to cut in two   bi _ _ _ _

2. a seeking   q _ _ _ _

3. a mixture of cereal, nuts, and fruit
   served for breakfast   _ _ _ _ ola

4. fellow-feeling   com _ _ _ _ ion

5. to bubble   ef _ _ _ _ esce

6. place where grain is stored   _ _ _ _ ary

7. a break   _ _ _ _ _ ure

8. lacking feeling or emotion   im _ _ _ _ ive

9. the smaller part   _ _ _ _ _ ity

10. a doctor's client   _ _ _ _ ent

5. Words of Interest. Supply the appropriate word from the list below.

1. "voting with shards": the right to vote   _____

2. an invertebrate with sharply marked
   body features   _____

3. gemstone   _____

4. shell filled with explosives   _____

5. "bone-crusher": fish-eating hawk   _____

6. ornamental work of delicate design   _____

7. "seedy apple": a fruit containing many seeds _____

8. slow, stately dance   _____

9. tool that cuts tall grass   _____

10. of special excellence or beauty   _____

11. medieval musician   _____

12. detailed list of entrees   _____

exquisite	insect	osprey
filigree	menu	pomegranate
garnet	minstrel	sickle
grenade	minuet	suffrage

6. Indicate whether each statement is true or false by circling T or F.

T   F   1. *Villain* originally signified a farm laborer.

T   F   2. Etymologically, *commencement* exercises celebrate the beginning of a graduate's career.

T   F   3. A *saturnine* temperament is characterized by unpredictable changes of mood.

T   F   4. The *-cle* in *monocle* is a diminutive suffix.

T   F   5. Although *perish* and *decedent* derive from different Latin bases, they share the idea of permanent departure.

T   F   6. *Liquor* once referred to any liquid.

T   F   7. *Gladiolus* means "little sword."

T   F   8. The drink *sangría* is named for its blood-red color.

T   F   9. The etymology of *disaster* is "ill-starred."

T   F   10. *Refrain* (to hold back) derives from the Latin base FRANG-.

7. Review: Occupations. Match each word with the base from which it derives.

____ 1. journalist	A. ART-
____ 2. courier	B. CAP-, (CIP-), CAPT-, (CEPT-)
____ 3. director	C. CUR(R)-, CURS-
____ 4. advocate	D. [JOURN-]
____ 5. executive	E. DUC-, DUCT-
____ 6. artist	F. EQU-, (IQU-)
____ 7. minister	G. FIRM-
____ 8. farmer	H. JUDIC-
____ 9. equilibrist	I. MINOR-, MINUS-, MINUT-
____ 10. caterer	J. PON-, POSIT-
____ 11. producer	K. REG-, (RIG-), RECT-
____ 12. composer	L. SEN-
____ 13. senator	M. SERV-
____ 14. judge	N. SEQU-, SECUT-
____ 15. conservator	O. VOC-, VOK-

8. Review: Supply the missing base.

1. truthfulness   _ _ _ acity

2. like   _ _ _ _ _ ar

3. lively   _ _ _ acious

4. friendship, especially among nations   _ _ ity

5. readable   _ _ _ ible

6. "on the dot"   _ _ _ _ _ ual

7. forewarning   pre _ _ _ ition

8. care of the hands   mani _ _ _ e

9. fatherly   _ _ _ _ _ _ al

10. to go out   ex _ _

11. the act of speaking alone   _ _ _ iloquy

12. sharp   _ _ _ te

13. motherhood   _ _ _ _ _ _ ity

14. capable of being touched   _ _ _ _ ible

15. to ask   in _ _ _ _ e

9. Review: Complete each statement by supplying the meaning of the base.

1. The base in *prenatal, nativity,* and *Renaissance* means _____.

2. The base in *fable, preface,* and *infant* means _____.

3. The base in *grade, ingredient,* and *graduate* means _____.

4. The base in *distort, torch,* and *tortuous* means _____.

5. The base in *lever, carnival,* and *alleviate* means _____.

6. The base in *canary, incentive,* and *chant* means _____.

7. The base in *pensive, pound,* and *ponder* means _____.

8. The base in *cabbage, cadet,* and *capital* means _____.

9. The base in *cadaver, cascade,* and *accident* means _____.

10. The base in *foreclose, exclusive,* and *occlusion* means _____.

10. Review: The words in this exercise have entered English through Italian. Match each word with the base from which it derives.

_____ 1. segue		A. CAD-, (CID-), CAS-
_____ 2. cadenza		B. CRE-, CRESC-, CRET-
_____ 3. novella		C. DE-, DIV-
_____ 4. replica		D. FAC-, (FIC-), FACT-, (FECT-)
_____ 5. tempo		E. FLU-, FLUX-, FLUOR(O)-, FLUV-
_____ 6. influenza		F. FOLI-
_____ 7. umbrella		G. NOV-
_____ 8. diva		H. PLIC-, PLEX-
_____ 9. confetti		I. PUNG-, PUNCT-
_____ 10. improvisatore		J. SEQU-, SECUT-
_____ 11. solo		K. SOL-
_____ 12. portfolio		L. TEMPER-, TEMPOR-
_____ 13. terra cotta		M. TERR-
_____ 14. crescendo		N. UMBR- (shade)
_____ 15. contrapuntal		O. VID-, VIS-

LESSON XVIII

1. Indicate whether the following pairs are synonyms or antonyms by circling S or A.

S	A	1. dictum	-	maxim
S	A	2. valiant	-	cowardly
S	A	3. agile	-	awkward
S	A	4. clamorous	-	vociferous
S	A	5. edict	-	proclamation
S	A	6. consonance	-	discord
S	A	7. predicament	-	dilemma
S	A	8. conditional	-	provisional
S	A	9. prodigal	-	frugal
S	A	10. conscientious	-	painstaking
S	A	11. prevalent	-	scarce
S	A	12. cogitate	-	ponder
S	A	13. congeries	-	aggregation
S	A	14. resonant	-	orotund
S	A	15. redaction	-	revision

2. GER-, GEST-

Match each word with the best definition.*

_____	1. congest	A. to propose
_____	2. digest	B. to excrete
_____	3. egest	C. to assimilate
_____	4. ingest	D. to overcrowd
_____	5. suggest	E. to take in by swallowing

*The nouns that correspond to these verbs end in -gestion: *congestion*, *digestion*, etc.; *digest* can function as both noun and verb.

3. DIC-, DICT-; MIT(T)-, MIS(S)-; VAL-, [VAIL-]

Match each word with the best definition.

____ 1. contradiction		A. to reduce the worth of
____ 2. condition		B. denial; inconsistency
____ 3. ditto (v.)		C. priceless
____ 4. prediction		D. to make use of
____ 5. submit		E. death
____ 6. demise		F. the process of recovering one's health
____ 7. noncommittal		G. sound; effective
____ 8. premise		H. a lessening of degree
____ 9. remission		I. stipulation
____ 10. convalescence		J. a foretelling
____ 11. ambivalent		K. to yield to another
____ 12. avail		L. to duplicate
____ 13. devalue		M. not having a particular view
____ 14. invaluable		N. proposition supporting a conclusion
____ 15. valid		O. simultaneously attracted to and repulsed from

4. Words of Interest. Supply the appropriate word from the list below.

Word	Etymological Meaning	Current Meaning
1. _____	the act of speaking ill of	a curse
2. _____	Christian martyr	sentimental card sent on February 14th
3. _____	driving in both directions	capable of multiple meanings
4. _____	waging war	hostile
5. _____	a saying farewell	farewell address at commencement
6. _____	wordbook	lexicon

7. _____ what is put on the table untidy condition

8. _____ to beat with a club to criticize harshly

9. _____ something truly said decision of a jury

10. _____ deed; exploit joke; taunt

11. _____ to release from one's hand to free from bondage

12. _____ something sent communication through an intermediary

13. _____ to drive a ship to traverse the sea or air

14. _____ someone in poor health an invalid

15. _____ little song poem of 14 lines

ambiguous	malediction	register
belligerent	manumit	sonnet
dictionary	mess	valediction
fustigate	message	valentine
gerund	navigate	valetudinarian
jest	predict	verdict

5. CLAM-, [CLAIM-]

Match each word with the best definition.*

____ 1. acclaim   A. to renounce

____ 2. declaim   B. to recover lost articles

____ 3. disclaim   C. to interject

____ 4. exclaim   D. to announce publicly

____ 5. proclaim   E. to applaud enthusiastically

____ 6. reclaim   F. to recite for rhetorical effect

*The nouns that correspond to these verbs end in -clamation: *acclamation*, *declamation*, etc.; *acclaim* can function as both noun and verb.

6. Word Analysis. For each word, circle the letter of the correct analysis.

1. compromise:
   - (A) with/through/to send/n.
   - (B) against/through/to send/adj.
   - (C) with/forward/to send/n.
   - (D) against/forward/to send/adj.

2. omniscient:
   - (A) all/to know/n.
   - (B) all/to know/adj.
   - (C) all/to have power/adj.
   - (D) all/to have power/n.

3. soniferous:
   - (A) sound/to make/v.
   - (B) sound/to make/n.
   - (C) sound/to bear, carry/n.
   - (D) sound/to bear, carry/adj.

4. ambiguity:
   - (A) to love/twice/to drive/n.
   - (B) to love/twice/to drive/adj.
   - (C) both/to drive/n.
   - (D) both/to drive/adj.

5. dedicate:
   - (A) apart, in different directions/to say/n.
   - (B) apart, in different directions/to teach/n.
   - (C) down, thoroughly/to teach/v.
   - (D) down, thoroughly/to say/v.

6. valedictory:
   - (A) farewell/to speak/adj.
   - (B) truth/to lead/adj.
   - (C) farewell/to lead/n.
   - (D) truth/to speak/adj.

7. manumission:
   - (A) to remind/to send/v.
   - (B) to remind/to send/n.
   - (C) hand/to send/v.
   - (D) hand/to send/n.

8. belligerence:
   - (A) beauty/flock/n.
   - (B) beauty/to carry, produce/n.
   - (C) war/flock/n.
   - (D) war/to carry, produce/n.

9. effervesce:
   - (A) from/to boil, bubble/v.
   - (B) from/to boil, bubble/n.
   - (C) from/to bear, carry/n.
   - (D) from/to bear, carry/v.

10. equivalent:
   - (A) horse/worth/adj.
   - (B) horse/worth/n.
   - (C) equal/worth/adj.
   - (D) equal/worth/n.

7. Review: Indicate whether each statement is true or false by circling T or F.

T   F   1. Euphemisms are seldom employed for words and expressions associated with death.

T   F   2. The etymological meaning of *lavatory* is "a place for washing."

T   F   3. *Sanctimonious* has undergone elevation of meaning.

T   F   4. A *vitamin* is a substance "essential to life."

T   F   5. *Sonar* is an acronym for "so[und] na[vigation and] r[anging]."

T   F   6. *Patronize* can mean "to act condescendingly toward."

T F 7. *Fumigate* and *perfume* both derive from the Latin base for "smoke."

T F 8. The etymology of *chaplain* is "keeper of the rosary."

T F 9. Originally, a *count* served as a companion to a king.

T F 10. *Senate* owes its derivation to the fact that this Roman council originally was composed of elders.

8. **Review:** Circle the letter of the one word in each group that is <u>not</u> similar in meaning to the other three.

1. (A) doctrine
   (B) principle
   (C) tenet
   (D) subsidy

2. (A) dissonant
   (B) dissolute
   (C) perverted
   (D) unprincipled

3. (A) appendage
   (B) accessory
   (C) attraction
   (D) adjunct

4. (A) enjoin
   (B) direct
   (C) order
   (D) elucidate

5. (A) sinecure
   (B) entertainment
   (C) distraction
   (D) diversion

6. (A) coincident
   (B) adventitious
   (C) simultaneous
   (D) contemporaneous

7. (A) edict
   (B) predicament
   (C) proclamation
   (D) decree

8. (A) controvert
   (B) separate
   (C) divide
   (D) disjoin

9. (A) prejudice
   (B) preconception
   (C) prepossession
   (D) preview

10. (A) envoy
    (B) courier
    (C) messenger
    (D) corsair

11. (A) succeed
    (B) supervene
    (C) ensue
    (D) cant

12. (A) definite
    (B) submissive
    (C) compliant
    (D) tractable

13. (A) ambiguous
    (B) equivocal
    (C) ambitious
    (D) uncertain

14. (A) exquisite
    (B) refined
    (C) valetudinary
    (D) elegant

15. (A) frail
    (B) fractious
    (C) rebellious
    (D) contentious

16. (A) summon
    (B) convoke
    (C) assemble
    (D) declaim

17. (A) aspect
    (B) feature
    (C) facet
    (D) vista

18. (A) sudden
    (B) abstruse
    (C) unexpected
    (D) rapid

9. Review: Food and Drink. Match each word with the base from which it derives.

____ 1. aquavit		A. AC(U)-, ACR-, ACET-
____ 2. flambé		B. AQU(A)-
____ 3. mincemeat		C. BENE-, BON-
____ 4. divinity		D. CAP-, (CIP-), CAPT-, (CEPT-)
____ 5. grains		E. CRE-, CRESC-, CRET-
____ 6. parfait		F. DE-, DIV-
____ 7. vinegar		G. FAC-, (FIC-), FACT-, (FECT-)
____ 8. legumes		H. FLAG(R)-, FLAM(M)-
____ 9. cauliflower		I. FLOR-
____ 10. compote		J. GRAN-
____ 11. sauté		K. LEG-, (LIG-), LECT-
____ 12. catered		L. MINOR-, MINUS-, MINUT-
____ 13. bonbons		M. PAN- (bread)
____ 14. panettone		N. PON-, POSIT-
____ 15. croissant		O. SAL-, (SIL-), SALT-, (SULT-)

LESSON XIX

1. <u>SCRIB-, SCRIPT-</u>

Match each word with the best definition.*

_____ 1. ascribe	A. to condemn; to prohibit
_____ 2. circumscribe	B. to make a written copy of
_____ 3. conscript	C. to attribute
_____ 4. describe	D. to engrave; to autograph
_____ 5. inscribe	E. to append one's signature to a document
_____ 6. prescribe	F. to enroll for military service
_____ 7. proscribe	G. to give an account of
_____ 8. subscribe	H. to delimit; to encircle
_____ 9. superscribe	I. to write above or on top of
_____ 10. transcribe	J. to designate the use of a remedy

*The nouns that correspond to these verbs end in -script or -scription: *ascription*, *circumscription*, *conscript*, *conscription*, etc.

2. Indicate whether the following pairs are synonyms or antonyms by circling S or A.

S	A	1. rest	-	remainder
S	A	2. constant	-	variable
S	A	3. statute	-	edict
S	A	4. nominal	-	significant
S	A	5. exist	-	occur
S	A	6. erratic	-	unconventional
S	A	7. destiny	-	fate
S	A	8. persistent	-	obstinate
S	A	9. convoluted	-	difficult
S	A	10. extant	-	extinct
S	A	11. objective	-	impartial
S	A	12. instate	-	dismiss
S	A	13. abject	-	despicable
S	A	14. revolve	-	rotate
S	A	15. stationary	-	movable

111

3. Words of Interest. Supply the appropriate word from the list below.

Word	Etymological Meaning	Current Meaning
1. _____	a stopping place	unit of verse
2. _____	a calling by name	system of naming
3. _____	a roll of writing	one book within a set
4. _____	something thrown	a casting of goods overboard
5. _____	to write too much	to write in a careless, hurried manner
6. _____	a naming again	celebrity; fame
7. _____	a staying of arms	truce
8. _____	small object that stands in the way	hindrance
9. _____	a standing over	belief unreasonably supported by faith in magic or chance
10. _____	something written afterward	message appended to the end of a letter
11. _____	a turn-face	a reversal; about-face
12. _____	war name	pseudonym
13. _____	rolled together	intricate; complicated
14. _____	a little place for standing	lodging for horses and cattle
15. _____	to stand with or firm	to have as a price

armistice	obstacle	stable
convoluted	postscript	stanza
cost	renown	steadfast
jettison	scribble	superstition
nom de guerre	scripture	volte-face
nomenclature	solstice	volume

4. In the following two exercises, match each word with the best definition.

ST(A)-, STIT-, SIST-

____	1. constitution	A. poverty-stricken
____	2. destitute	B. an established body of laws; physique
____	3. institute	C. to replace
____	4. restitution	D. to establish
____	5. substitute	E. restoration of things to their rightful owner or previous state

____	1. assist	A. to cease
____	2. consist	B. to oppose
____	3. desist	C. to be composed of
____	4. insist	D. to live, as on food
____	5. resist	E. to stand by to help
____	6. subsist*	F. to assert firmly

*Other SIST- verbs that follow this pattern include *exist* and *persist*. The nouns that correspond to these verbs end in -ance, -ence, or -ency: *assistance, consistence, consistency*, etc.

5. Indicate whether each statement is true or false by circling T of F.

T   F   1. *Stanza* derives from the base ST(A)-.

T   F   2. *Carnival* = "farewell to meat" is an example of a popular etymology.

T   F   3. The words *male* and *female* are linguistically related.

T   F   4. A *stallion* is so called because it <u>st</u>ands in a <u>st</u>all in a <u>st</u>able.

T   F   5. *Jet* (aircraft) ultimately derives from the base JECT-.

T   F   6. *Religious* and *sacrilegious* are etymologically unrelated.

T   F   7. The spelling of *cockroach* has been unaffected by folk etymology.

T   F   8. A *namesake* is a person named in honor of another.

T   F   9. The verb *err* also may be used as a noun.

T   F   10. The words *pounce* and *pronounce* both belong to the NOMIN-family of words.

6. <u>ERR-; JAC-, JECT-; SCRIB-, SCRIPT-; ST(A)-, STIT-, SIST-; VOLV-, VOLUT-</u>

Match each word with the best definition.

____ 1. errata	A. large; full
____ 2. aberration	B. a room for valuables
____ 3. projectile	C. to attribute to a specific source
____ 4. trajectory	D. majestic
____ 5. jut	E. to unfold; to develop
____ 6. ascribe	F. remaining
____ 7. script	G. deviation from the normal
____ 8. restaurant	H. to detain in legal custody
____ 9. arrest	I. list of errors
____ 10. stately	J. incident; occurrence
____ 11. circumstance	K. a chosen course
____ 12. evolve	L. to protrude
____ 13. voluble	M. a place that serves meals
____ 14. vault	N. talkative; glib
____ 15. voluminous	O. missile
	P. the written text of a play, for example

7. <u>JAC-, JECT-</u>

Match each word with the best definition.*

____ 1. conjecture	A. to introduce into; to intrude
____ 2. deject	B. to throw forward; to predict
____ 3. eject	C. to dishearten
____ 4. interject	D. to throw out; to expel
____ 5. object	E. to rebuff; to discard as useless
____ 6. project	F. to cause to undergo something; to subjugate
____ 7. reject	G. to disapprove; to oppose
____ 8. subject	H. to guess

*The nouns that correspond to these verbs end in -ject or -jection, with the exception of *conjecture*.

REVIEW OF LESSONS XV–XIX (SELF-TESTING: Answers can be found in Appendix C.)

1. Indicate whether each statement is true or false by circling T of F.

T   F   1. A very *superstitious* person is unlikely to leave the house for the duration of Friday the 13th.

T   F   2. As an adjective, *invalid* (not valid) is accented on the second syllable; as a noun, *invalid* (a sickly person) is accented on the first syllable.

T   F   3. Etymologically, the noun *acrimony* means "sharp warning."

T   F   4. The word *homicide* may be used to describe both the crime and its perpetrator.

T   F   5. *Sanguine* is one of several words whose current meaning derives from the humeral theory of physiology.

T   F   6. Originally, *obstetrician* meant "midwife."

T   F   7. *Awful* always has been used in the sense of "very bad" or "dreadful."

T   F   8. A querulous *valetudinarian* is an ideal hospital patient for an inexperienced nursing student.

T   F   9. *Suffragette* and *frail* derive from different Latin bases.

T   F   10. *Legumes* derive their name from the fact that they are "collectibles."

T   F   11. The word *victuals* is pronounced as if it were spelled "vittles."

T   F   12. The word *minutiae* refers to trifling details.

T   F   13. The origin of *ambition* goes back to the Roman political system: candidates for office would "go around [seeking votes]."

T   F   14. The word *jest*, which once referred to any tale, has undergone specialization of meaning; it now means "witty tale."

T   F   15. *Invaluable* and *valuable* mean exactly the same thing.

2. Supply the missing base.

1. handwritten (text)   manu _ _ _ _ _

2. lifelike   _ _ _ id

3. motherly   m _ _ _ _ al

4. to name ___ ___ ___ ___ ___ ate

5. to foretell pre ___ ___ ___ ___

6. of equal worth equi ___ ___ ___ ent

7. foreknowledge pre ___ ___ ___ ence

8. breakable ___ ___ ___ ___ ___ ible

9. having a deep sound ___ ___ ___ orous

10. penman s ___ ___ ___ ___ e

11. very small m ___ ___ ___ ___ e

12. growing ___ ___ ___ ___ cent

13. state of being alone ___ ___ ___ itude

14. to withdraw from the fatherland ex ___ ___ ___ ___ ___ ate

15. a warning ad ___ ___ ___ ition

3. Crime, Death, and Punishment. Match each word with the base from which it derives.

____ 1. commit	A. CID-, CIS-	
____ 2. arrest	B. DIC-, DICT-	
____ 3. uxoricide	C. JAC-, JECT-	
____ 4. inquest	D. MIT(T)-, MIS(S)-	
____ 5. perpetrate	E. MON-	
____ 6. indictment	F. PATR-, PATERN-	
____ 7. proscription	G. QUIR-, QUISIT-, QUEST-	
____ 8. [lethal] injection	H. SCRIB-, SCRIPT-	
____ 9. summons	I. SEQU-, SECUT-	
____ 10. execution	J. ST(A)-, STIT-, SIST-	

4. Indicate whether the following pairs are synonyms or antonyms by circling S or A.

S	A	1. absolve	-	exonerate
S	A	2. increase	-	reduction
S	A	3. cogent	-	compelling
S	A	4. subsequent	-	prior
S	A	5. dispassionate	-	biased
S	A	6. persistent	-	tenacious
S	A	7. register	-	roster
S	A	8. fermentation	-	unrest
S	A	9. proffer	-	tender
S	A	10. itinerant	-	nomadic
S	A	11. evolve	-	develop
S	A	12. subjugate	-	conquer
S	A	13. aberrant	-	normal
S	A	14. constant	-	changeable
S	A	15. decisive	-	inconclusive

5. Word Analysis. Identify the prefix (if any) and the base in each word and then give the meaning of each element.

	PREFIX	BASE
1. premise	_____	_____
2. dissonance	_____	_____
3. executrix	_____	_____
4. ambivalence	_____	_____
5. clamor	_____	_____
6. accretion	_____	_____
7. inquiry	_____	_____

	PREFIX	BASE
8. agility	_____	_____
9. granule	_____	_____
10. vivacity	_____	_____
11. patrimony	_____	_____
12. circumstance	_____	_____
13. monitor	_____	_____
14. projectile	_____	_____
15. segment	_____	_____
16. minuscule	_____	_____
17. obituary	_____	_____
18. compassion	_____	_____
19. revolutionary	_____	_____
20. fracture	_____	_____

LESSON XX

1. Give the unshortened form of the following clipped words.

1. brandy   _____   6. improv   _____

2. bus   _____   7. limo   _____

3. curio   _____   8. mob   _____

4. exam   _____   9. mutt   _____

5. hype   _____   10. zoo   _____

2. Try to supply the appropriate word before referring to the list of possible answers at the end of the exercise.

A. 1. A _____ is so called because of its edible root.

2. The word _____ reflects the fact that it once referred to a head covering.

3. The surface on which money is counted or business transacted is called a _____.

4. Etymologically, an officer who is "place-holding" is called a _____.

5. The person who is head of a kitchen is called a _____.

6. The etymological meaning of the verb _____ is "to prune on both sides"; its current meaning is "to remove limbs from the body."

7. Henry the VIII of England dispatched two of his wives by _____.

8. The engine that pushes or pulls a train is called a _____ because it "moves from place to place."

9. What people think of you, either good or bad, is called your _____.

10. If something has been _____, it has been "rooted out."

B. 1. A _____ is a vegetable that resembles the shape of a person's head.

2. The word _____ describes strong distilled liquor.

3. A woman wearing a disguise to conceal her identity is said to be _____.

4. A person who appreciates the subtleties of culture or the fine arts is called a _____.

5. A literary work furnished with explanatory notes is called an _____ edition.

6. An older person who attends a social gathering of young people to ensure that they behave properly is called a _____.

7. A person widely (but unfavorably) known as a result of criminal activities or outrageous behavior is termed _____.

8. A large, sleeveless outer garment is called a _____.

9. A person who is known to someone but is not a close friend is called an _____.

10. Something that possesses an old-fashioned attractiveness or that is pleasantly odd is described as _____.

A		B	
amputate	kerchief	acquaintance	connoisseur
chef	lieutenant	annotated	incognita
counter	locomotive	cabbage	notorious
decapitation	radish	cape	quaint
eradicated	reputation	chaperon	spirits

3. Circle the letter of the definition that best fits the underscored word or phrase.

1. to <u>recapitulate</u> the day's events: (A) consider (B) complete (C) summarize

2. to <u>reconnoiter</u> the enemy position: (A) attack (B) survey (C) lay siege

3. to <u>capitalize</u> on the situation: (A) benefit from (B) approve (C) take charge of

4. a <u>derogatory</u> remark: (A) questioning (B) disparaging   (C) arrogant

5. a <u>precipitous</u> cliff: (A) steep   (B) rocky   (C) wet

6. <u>in lieu of</u> flowers: (A) in the form of (B) similar to   (C) in place of

7. a teacher's <u>prerogative</u>: (A) privilege   (B) question   (C) criticism

8. a certain <u>esprit de corps</u>: (A) jocosity   (B) seductive quality (C) sense of unity

9. <u>couchant</u> lions: (A) attacking   (B) lying down   (C) ravenous

10. a <u>radical</u> change: (A) grass roots (B) influential   (C) extreme

11. to <u>abrogate</u> a law: (A) propose   (B) annul   (C) denounce

12. to <u>prorogue</u> the senate: (A) harangue   (B) suspend   (C) incite to riot

13. a <u>sprightly</u> octogenarian: (A) ethereal   (B) lively   (C) asthmatic

14. to <u>discount</u> the story: (A) narrate   (B) recollect   (C) disregard

15. a <u>surrogate</u> mother: (A) substitute   (B) abusive   (C) overly affectionate

4. In the following three exercises, match each word with the best definition.

<u>SPIR-*</u>

_____ 1. aspire	A. to sweat	
_____ 2. conspire	B. to breathe in and out	
_____ 3. expire	C. to come to light	
_____ 4. inspire	D. to seek to attain	
_____ 5. perspire	E. to die	
_____ 6. respire	F. to plot against	
_____ 7. transpire	G. to breathe into: to communicate by divine influence	

*The nouns that correspond to these verbs end in -(s)piration: *aspiration, conspiration,* etc. In addition, *conspire* has the noun-form *conspiracy* and *expire, expiry*.

LOC-*

____ 1. allocation	A. the act of moving to a new place
____ 2. collocation	B. displacement
____ 3. dislocation	C. the act of placing together
____ 4. location	D. distribution
____ 5. relocation	E. place; position

*The verbs that correspond to these nouns end in -locate: *allocate*, *collocate*, etc.

PUT-**

____ 1. compute	A. to accuse; to attribute something discreditable
____ 2. depute	
____ 3. dispute	B. to argue
____ 4. impute	C. to calculate
____ 5. repute	D. to consider; to deem
	E. to appoint as an agent

**The nouns that correspond to these verbs end in -putation: *computation*, *deputation*, etc. In addition, the verbs *dispute* and *repute* have analogous noun-forms, *dispute* and *repute*.

5. Review: Indicate whether the following pairs are synonyms or antonyms by circling S or A.

S	A	1. interjection	-	exclamation
S	A	2. capricious	-	steadfast
S	A	3. unconscionable	-	excessive
S	A	4. notion	-	idea
S	A	5. postpone	-	suspend
S	A	6. recount	-	narrate
S	A	7. ambivalent	-	certain
S	A	8. sever	-	join
S	A	9. predominant	-	prevalent
S	A	10. achieve	-	fail

6. Review: In the following two exercises, match each word with the best definition.

_____ 1. regicide	A. applause
_____ 2. retentive	B. killer of a king
_____ 3. captivate	C. bitter; sarcastic
_____ 4. sedentary	D. to bewitch
_____ 5. cohabitate	E. obstruction
_____ 6. acclaim	F. requiring much sitting
_____ 7. impediment	G. page of a book numbered on one side only
_____ 8. folio	H. having a good memory
_____ 9. firmament	I. heavens
_____ 10. acrimonious	J. to live together

_____ 1. veridical	A. united into one body
_____ 2. incorporated	B. short-lived
_____ 3. strict	C. truthful
_____ 4. unconscionable	D. childish
_____ 5. resolute	E. determined
_____ 6. repulsive	F. contiguous
_____ 7. adjoining	G. severe; precise
_____ 8. infantile	H. fabled
_____ 9. legendary	I. lacking scruples
_____ 10. transient	J. disgusting

7. Review: Indicate the correct answer by circling A or B.

1. obsessive: (A) impulsive   (B) compulsive

2. pertinent: (A) apposite   (B) opposite

3. to torment: (A) persecute   (B) prosecute

4. stubborn: (A) perverse   (B) perverted

5. believable: (A) credible   (B) credulous

6. projectile: (A) missal   (B) missile

7. circumspect: (A) discrete   (B) discreet

8. brilliant: (A) ingenious   (B) ingenuous

8. Review: Business. Match each word with its <u>etymological</u> meaning.

____ 1. depository	A. terms drawn up
____ 2. affluent	B. to argue over a set of ten hides
____ 3. dicker	C. job without care
____ 4. amortize	D. a person who believes or trusts
____ 5. firm	E. overflowing [with wealth]
____ 6. sinecure	F. [money] that comes back
____ 7. deficit	G. a fixed business
____ 8. creditor	H. to make one
____ 9. manager	I. it is lacking
____ 10. revenue	J. sum or share to be divided
____ 11. contract	K. place for money to be set aside
____ 12. corporation	L. handler
____ 13. dividend	M. free from debt
____ 14. unionize	N. a body
____ 15. solvent	O. to extinguish a debt

LESSON XXI

1. <u>AL-, ALT-; MEDI-; MIGR-; MORT-; PET-; PROL-; PUG(N)-</u>

Match each word with the best definition.

_____	1. exalt	A. rival
_____	2. enhance	B. an average
_____	3. coalescence	C. deathless
_____	4. mean	D. undertaker
_____	5. media	E. repulsive
_____	6. transmigration	F. to intensify
_____	7. emigrate	G. passage of the soul into another body at death
_____	8. mortician	H. request
_____	9. immortal	I. productive
_____	10. rigor mortis	J. to leave one country for another
_____	11. competitor	K. to praise
_____	12. petition	L. inclined to fight
_____	13. prolific	M. blend; fusion
_____	14. pugnacious	N. rigidity of muscles after death
_____	15. repugnant	O. the means of communication that reach large numbers of people

2. Indicate whether each statement is true or false by circling T or F.

T   F   1. *Moratorium* is another word for funeral home.

T   F   2. The nouns *medium* (one who presides at a séance) and *intermediary* share the idea of "acting as a go-between."

T   F   3. A *petulant* person is one who makes a formal request.

T   F   4. *Mitt* is a clipped form of *mitten* (MEDI-).

T   F   5. A *pugilist* is a person who fights with the fists.

T   F   6. A *mezzo-soprano* is a mediocre singer.

T   F   7. Informally, the word *medieval* may refer to anything old-fashioned.

T   F   8. The word *meld* is an example of a blend, one combining *melt* and *weld*.

T   F   9. Etymologically, an *altar* is an elevated place.

T   F   10. The expression *memento mori* can refer to any reminder of death or human failings.

3. Words of Interest. Supply the appropriate word from the list below.

Word	Etymological Meaning	Current Meaning
1. _____	midway up the hill	ordinary
2. _____	to put to death	to humiliate
3. _____	a citizen contributing to the state only by producing offspring	working class
4. _____	to fight against	to attack with words
5. _____	a floor between floors	an intermediate story that protrudes in the form of a balcony
6. _____	a promise to pay in the event of a person's death	the conveyance of property to a creditor
7. _____	something that stimulates the desire to eat	a canapé, for example
8. _____	the middle	the means of communication that reach a wide audience
9. _____	a disease that attacks	a contagious skin disease
10. _____	having nothing in the middle	instant; direct
11. _____	nourishment	support paid by a spouse following a divorce
12. _____	high; lofty	snobbish; arrogant

alimony	impetus	migrant
appetizer	impugn	morbidity
haughty	media	mortgage
immediate	mediocre	mortify
impetigo	mezzanine	proletariat

4. Review: Indicate whether the following pairs are synonyms or antonyms by circling S or A.

S	A	1. aver	-	affirm
S	A	2. versed	-	unfamiliar
S	A	3. dilatory	-	prompt
S	A	4. exquisite	-	refined
S	A	5. predicament	-	dilemma
S	A	6. remiss	-	conscientious
S	A	7. refrain	-	chorus
S	A	8. devolution	-	degeneration
S	A	9. precipitous	-	flat
S	A	10. provenience	-	origin
S	A	11. adore	-	worship
S	A	12. connoisseur	-	amateur
S	A	13. quaint	-	ordinary
S	A	14. cape	-	promontory
S	A	15. incompatible	-	disagreeable

5. Review: The words in this exercise have verb-forming suffixes. Supply the missing base.

1. to make strong   _ _ _ _ ify

2. to put in the same order   co _ _ _ _ _ ate

3. to name   _ _ _ _ _ ate

4. to "get in the way of": to avert   ob _ _ ate

5. to make right   _ _ _ _ ify

6. to pay   com _ _ _ _ ate

7. to enlarge   _ _ _ _ ify

8. to enlighten; to explain   e _ _ _ idate

9. to "become strong": to recover from an illness   con _ _ _ esce

10. to establish the truth of   _ _ _ ify

11. to make thin; to weaken   at _ _ _ _ ate

12. to make into one   _ _ ify

13. to make heavy: to make worse   ag _ _ _ _ ate

14. to behead   de _ _ _ _ _ ate

15. to bring to nothing; to invalidate   _ _ _ _ ify

16. to make a god of   _ _ ify

17. to put to death on a cross   _ _ _ _ ify

18. to make light; to relieve   al _ _ _ iate

19. to question formally   inter _ _ _ ate

20. to make sacred   con _ _ _ _ ate

LESSON XXII

1. Use a check to indicate each pair of doublets.

____	1. confuse	-	confound
____	2. complicate	-	compound
____	3. cruise	-	cross
____	4. matron	-	patron
____	5. perfect	-	parfait
____	6. deceased	-	departed
____	7. dignity	-	dainty
____	8. regal	-	kingly
____	9. recapitulation	-	precipitous
____	10. deity	-	diva

2. Indicate whether each statement is true or false by circling T or F.

T   F   1. Most authors are delighted when school administrators *expurgate* passages from their literary work.

T   F   2. *Purgatory* is a place where one's sins are cleansed.

T   F   3. A person who performs a service *gratis* expects a big tip.

T   F   4. *Vulgarism* and *Vulgate* (the Latin translation of the Bible) share the same base.

T   F   5. *Miscellanea* and *potpourri* are synonyms.

T   F   6. A *natatorium* is a nursery for newborns.

T   F   7. The etymological meaning of *meddle* is "to mix" into someone else's business.

T   F   8. A *doublet* refers to two or more words in the same language that enter by different routes of transmission from the same source.

T   F   9. If someone serves a dish called a *medley*, it contains a *mélange* of ingredients.

T   F   10. The word *deny* ultimately derives from the Latin base NEG-.

3. GRAT-; MISC-, MIXT-; NEG-; PURG-; VULG-

Match each word with the best definition.

____	1. disgrace	A. common
____	2. agreeable	B. to declare publicly
____	3. congratulate	C. indiscriminate
____	4. grace	D. to cleanse; to eliminate
____	5. ingratiate	E. self-denial
____	6. gratuity	F. to gain the favor of others
____	7. promiscuous	G. to honor; to adorn
____	8. medley	H. spotless
____	9. mixture	I. dishonor
____	10. negate	J. to nullify
____	11. abnegation	K. anything having two or more diverse elements
____	12. purge	L. a tip
____	13. pure	M. to express joy over someone's achievement
____	14. vulgar	N. congenial
____	15. promulgate	O. musical "mixture" of passages taken from other compositions

4. Words of Interest. Supply the appropriate word from the list below.

	Word	Etymological Meaning	Current Meaning
1.	_____	purely blind	obtuse
2.	_____	common	crude
3.	_____	gratitude	elegance of motion
4.	_____	to deny again	to go back on a promise
5.	_____	to make common	to disclose
6.	_____	mixed-mixed	hasty or confused
7.	_____	a deserter of religious faith	traitor

8. _____ of mixed race   a person of mixed blood

9. _____ purified; strained   a cooked and sieved food

10. _____ the changeable common people   a disorderly or lawless crowd

divulge	miscellany	purée
grace	mob	renegade
melee	pell-mell	renege
mestizo	purblind	vulgar

5. MOBIL-, MOV-, MOT-

Supply the appropriate word from the list below.

1. cinema   _____

2. recurrent movement or theme   _____

3. not movable; fixed   _____

4. a lowering in rank   _____

5. elevation in rank   _____

6. to disband   _____

7. an instant of time   _____

8. disturbance; confusion   _____

9. movable   _____

10. impetus behind a crime or action   _____

11. self-propelled vehicle   _____

12. a strong, subjective feeling   _____

13. far removed; secluded   _____

14. rebellion _____

15. incentive _____

automobile	immobile	motive
commotion	mobile	movies
demobilize	moment	mutiny
demotion	motif	promotion
emotion	motivation	remote

6. Review: Indicate the correct answer by circling A or B.

1. incapable of being solved: (A) insolvent   (B) insoluble

2. to misrepresent: (A) contort   (B) distort

3. truthful: (A) veracious   (B) voracious

4. inflicting extreme pain: (A) torturous   (B) tortuous

5. to deduce: (A) infer   (B) imply

6. graphic: (A) vivacious   (B) vivid

7. to examine: (A) prove   (B) probe

8. to supply with light: (A) elucidate   (B) illuminate

9. authorized: (A) official   (B) officious

10. a direction to a pharmacist: (A) proscription   (B) prescription

11. aware: (A) conscientious   (B) conscious

12. enunciation: (A) diction   (B) dictation

13. an ornament: (A) pensive   (B) pendant

14. urgent: (A) exigent   (B) exiguous

15. slight: (A) negligible   (B) negligent

LESSON XXIII

1. PORT-

Match each word with the best definition.*

_____ 1. comportment   A. expulsion from a country
_____ 2. deportation   B. a detailed account of news
_____ 3. exportation   C. conduct; bearing
_____ 4. importation   D. act of furnishing evidence for or providing
_____ 5. purport   livelihood to
_____ 6. reportage   E. act of bringing in goods from a foreign
_____ 7. support   country for sale or trade
_____ 8. transport   F. rapture; ecstasy
                              G. an apparent purpose; significance
                              H. act of sending goods abroad for sale or trade

*The verbs that correspond to these nouns end in -port: *comport*, *deport*, etc.

2. Indicate whether the following pairs are synonyms or antonyms by circling S or A.

S	A	1. deflect	-	deviate
S	A	2. import	-	insignificance
S	A	3. convince	-	persuade
S	A	4. invincible	-	insurmountable
S	A	5. indeterminate	-	definite
S	A	6. destroy	-	exterminate
S	A	7. manifest	-	abstruse
S	A	8. mandatory	-	compulsory
S	A	9. flexible	-	rigid
S	A	10. demand	-	require
S	A	11. rapport	-	affinity
S	A	12. importunate	-	insistent
S	A	13. vanquish	-	defeat
S	A	14. terminate	-	initiate
S	A	15. reflective	-	pensive

3. Words of Interest. Supply the appropriate word from the list below.

	Word	Etymological Meaning	Current Meaning
1.	_____	little hand	handcuff
2.	_____	sliding gate	iron grating in a medieval castle that prevents passage
3.	_____	harbor	a sweet, red wine
4.	_____	a handful of men	shrewd management for one's own interests
5.	_____	to release from slavery	to liberate
6.	_____	blowing toward the harbor	favorable
7.	_____	cloak-carrier	large leather suitcase
8.	_____	to conquer completely	to demonstrate clearly
9.	_____	to work by hand	to work toward a predetermined goal
10.	_____	something struck by the hand	public declaration of intentions
11.	_____	harmony	portable musical instrument
12.	_____	animal accustomed to the hand	a large dog
13.	_____	end; boundary	a word peculiar to a specific group or activity
14.	_____	of the hand	customary way of acting
15.	_____	to mark off the boundaries	to decide

accordion	manifesto	porch
determine	manikin	port
emancipate	manipulation	portcullis
evince	manner	porter
manacle	mastiff	portmanteau
maneuver	opportune	term

4. STRU-, STRUCT-

Supply the appropriate word from the list below.

1. directions _____

2. any part of a building above the foundation _____

3. total devastation _____

4. the supporting part of a building _____

5. to build _____

6. tool _____

7. diligent; assiduous _____

8. to interpret; to explain _____

9. hindrance _____

10. promoting improvement _____

construct	destruction	obstruction
constructive	industrious	reconstruction
construe	instructions	substructure
destroy	instrument	superstructure

5. <u>CORD-</u>

Match each word with the best definition.

____ 1. courage		A. to dishearten
____ 2. cordial		B. consonant
____ 3. encourage		C. support on a hinged church seat
____ 4. discourage		D. to hearten
____ 5. discordant		E. valor
____ 6. accordant		F. harmony
____ 7. record (n.)		G. inconsonant
____ 8. core		H. the best performance documented
____ 9. concord		I. friendly
____ 10. misericord		J. the heart of the matter

6. Indicate whether each statement is true or false by circling T or F.

T F 1. The etymology of *manage* is "to train horses."

T F 2. *Amanuensis* and *manicurist* are synonymous terms.

T F 3. *Vincent* is an appropriate name for a man keen on winning.

T F 4. The etymology of *portfolio* is "a carrier for leaves (of paper)."

T F 5. A *portmanteau* word is restricted to terms and expressions having to do with travel.

T F 6. *Sport* is a clipped form of *disport*.

T F 7. In some schools, students are graded on their *deportment*.

T F 8. *Termite*, the wood-eating insect, derives from the base TERMIN-.

T F 9. The act of *manumission* dates back to ancient Rome, when masters sometimes freed their slaves.

T F 10. The etymology of *manufacture* is "to make by hand."

7. Review: Circle the letter of the one word in each group that is <u>not</u> similar in meaning to the other three.

1. (A) decimate
   (B) extort
   (C) exterminate
   (D) eradicate

2. (A) reputation
   (B) renown
   (C) infamy
   (D) fame

3. (A) inconsequential
   (B) trivial
   (C) incontinent
   (D) negligible

4. (A) achieve
   (B) attain
   (C) accomplish
   (D) aver

5. (A) sequential
   (B) extraordinary
   (C) noteworthy
   (D) exceptional

6. (A) submit
   (B) succumb
   (C) decapitate
   (D) capitulate

7. (A) reject
   (B) subscribe
   (C) disavow
   (D) repudiate

8. (A) compose
   (B) replicate
   (C) duplicate
   (D) reproduce

9. (A) rejoinder
   (B) retort
   (C) reply
   (D) repose

10. (A) enhance
    (B) reflect
    (C) intensify
    (D) embellish

11. (A) confirm
    (B) prove
    (C) confound
    (D) substantiate

12. (A) apposite
    (B) relevant
    (C) inconstant
    (D) pertinent

13. (A) dispassionate
    (B) equitable
    (C) objective
    (D) indigent

14. (A) vindicate
    (B) justify
    (C) pursue
    (D) absolve

15. (A) contort
    (B) efface
    (C) expunge
    (D) destroy

16. (A) diary
    (B) journal
    (C) descant
    (D) record

8. Review: Clothing. Match each word with the base from which it derives. (One base is used twice.)

_____ 1. apparel		A. CAPIT-, (CIPIT-)
_____ 2. lingerie		B. CORPOR-, CORP(US)-
_____ 3. vest		C. DU-
_____ 4. corset		D. FORT-
_____ 5. miniskirt		E. LEG-, (LIG-), LECT-
_____ 6. sombrero		F. LINE-
_____ 7. kerchief		G. MEDI-
_____ 8. suit		H. MINOR-, MINUS-, MINUT-
_____ 9. comforter		I. PAR-
_____ 10. negligee		J. PEND-, PENS-
_____ 11. cape		K. REG-, (RIG-), RECT-
_____ 12. dress		L. SEQU-, SECUT-
_____ 13. mittens		M. UMBR- (shade)
_____ 14. suspenders		N. VEST-
_____ 15. doublet		

9. Review: Indicate the correct answer by circling A or B.

1. incentive:	(A) motive	(B) motif
2. bury:	(A) inter	(B) enter
3. ornate:	(A) flagrant	(B) flamboyant
4. something that attracts:	(A) magnet	(B) magnate
5. injurious:	(A) noxious	(B) obnoxious
6. to kiss:	(A) osculate	(B) oscillate
7. manner:	(A) mode	(B) mold
8. biased:	(A) tenuous	(B) tendentious
9. skeptical:	(A) incredible	(B) incredulous
10. artificial:	(A) factious	(B) factitious

LESSON XXIV

1. Indicate whether the following pairs are synonyms or antonyms by circling S or A.

S	A	1. enunciation	-	diction
S	A	2. denounce	-	acclaim
S	A	3. satiety	-	deficiency
S	A	4. disobedient	-	compliant
S	A	5. impressive	-	grand
S	A	6. renounce	-	disclaim
S	A	7. impressionable	-	naïve
S	A	8. satisfied	-	discontented
S	A	9. announce	-	promulgate
S	A	10. appropriate	-	unseemly
S	A	11. audition	-	tryout
S	A	12. obeisance	-	homage
S	A	13. propriety	-	indecorum
S	A	14. pressure	-	stress
S	A	15. saturate	-	drench

2. PRESS-

Match each word with the best definition.*

____ 1. compress	A. to indicate one's feelings or opinions
____ 2. depress	B. to condense
____ 3. express	C. to subject someone to harsh authority
____ 4. impress	D. to keep from being published
____ 5. oppress	E. to discourage; to sadden
____ 6. repress	F. to influence favorably
____ 7. suppress	G. to hold back feelings in the subconscious

*The nouns that correspond to these verbs end in -press or -pression: *compress, compression, depression*, etc.

Part I, Lesson XXIV

3. Words of Interest. Supply the appropriate word from the list below.

1. to heed   _____

2. a literary genre   _____

3. messenger to the Pope   _____

4. media   _____

5. unhappy   _____

6. a traveling amusement show   _____

7. formal examination of records
   to check their accuracy   _____

8. "one's own": a piece of land   _____

9. rebirth of the soul in a new body   _____

10. entire property subject to payment
    of debts   _____

11. to rebuke severely   _____

12. a flesh-colored flower   _____

assets	nuncio	reincarnation
audit	obey	reprimand
carnation	press	sad
carnival	property	satire

4. Review: Circle the letter of the definition that best fits the underscored word.

1. to <u>mince</u> words: (A) moderate (B) mumble (C) misuse

2. a <u>tortuous</u> route: (A) painful   (B) winding   (C) hidden

3. a <u>patronizing</u> attitude: (A) condescending   (B) fatherly   (C) typical of one's ancestors

4. <u>terminal</u> cancer: (A) located in the extremities   (B) operable   (C) causing death

5. to <u>portage</u> a canoe: (A) paddle   (B) approach the dock from the left   (C) carry over land from one body of water to another

6. <u>adverse</u> weather: (A) hostile   (B) favorable   (C) fickle

7. an <u>incumbent</u> candidate: (A) presently holding office   (B) unlikely to win (C) likely to win

8. an <u>illuminated</u> manuscript: (A) medieval   (B) ahead of its time   (C) decorated with elaborate illustrations

9. <u>casualties</u> of war: (A) people lost   (B) happenings   (C) horrors

10. a <u>perfidious</u> friend: (A) faithful to a fault   (B) long-time   (C) disloyal

11. Yankee <u>ingenuity</u>:   (A) naïveté   (B) inventiveness   (C) conforming

12. <u>aberrant</u> behavior: (A) deviant   (B) convincing   (C) conforming

13. <u>tenuous</u> evidence: (A) insubstantial   (B) convincing   (C) massive

14. <u>plaited</u> hair: (A) braided   (B) thick   (C) dyed

15. a <u>semiannual</u> event: occurring   (A) every other year   (B) yearly   (C) twice a year

16. <u>specious</u> reasoning: (A) deceptive   (B) capacious   (C) logical

17. a <u>magnanimous</u> gesture: (A) cowardly   (B) noble   (C) emotional

18. <u>malicious</u> gossip: (A) false   (B) spiteful   (C) unjustified

19. <u>nefarious</u> deeds: (A) varied   (B) numerous   (C) evil

20. a <u>commuted</u> prison sentence: (A) exchanged for one less severe   (B) lengthened (C) unreasonably severe

21. <u>impending</u> disaster: (A) natural (B) unfortunate (C) imminent

22. to lead a <u>sedentary</u> life: (A) characterized by sitting   (B) rebellious   (C) nomadic

23. a <u>provocative</u> book: (A) obscene   (B) stimulating   (C) revealing

24. an <u>auspicious</u> occasion: (A) suggestive   (B) propitious   (C) unhappy

25. workmen's <u>compensation</u>:   (A) occupational hazard   (B) dues, as to a union (C) payment for injury

5. Review: Animals. Match each word with the base from which it derives.

____ 1. stallion	A. CANT-, (CENT-), [CHANT-]
____ 2. mastiff	B. CAPIT-, (CIPIT-)
____ 3. salmon	C. DOMIN-
____ 4. osprey	D. FLAG(R)-, FLAM(M)-
____ 5. dam	E. FRANG-, (FRING-), FRACT-
____ 6. cattle	F. MAN(U)-
____ 7. terrier	G. MISC-, MIXT-
____ 8. mustang	H. SAL-, (SIL-), SAL-, (SULT-)
____ 9. flamingo	I. ST(A)-, STIT-, SIST-
____ 10. chanticleer	J. TERR-

6. Review: Supply the missing letters to form an Anglo-Saxon equivalent of each Latinate word.

1. fort   s _ _ _ _ _ hold

2. grade (n.)   s _ _ _

3. injure   w _ _ _ _

4. gravity   h _ _ _ _ ness

5. optimum   b _ _ _

6. plenitude   f _ _ _ ness

7. primary   f _ _ _ _

8. sacred   h _ _ _

9. verbose   w _ _ _ y

10. vocation   c _ _ _ ing

11. unique   _ _ e [of a kind]

12. annual   _ _ _ _ ly

LESSON XXV

1. Give the plural(s) of each of the following nouns.

1. alumna   _____

2. alumnus   _____

3. atrium   _____

4. corpus   _____

5. crux   _____

6. datum   _____

7. index   _____

8. medium   _____

9. species   _____

10. stimulus   _____

2. Match each word with the best definition.

____ 1. opprobrium	A. gap
____ 2. quorum	B. customs; habits
____ 3. impetus	C. as
____ 4. interim	D. a majority
____ 5. mores	E. boredom
____ 6. lacuna	F. beyond what is seen or said
____ 7. qua	G. momentum
____ 8. tedium	H. disgrace
____ 9. ulterior	I. burden
____ 10. onus	J. interval

3. The words in the list below are Latin verbs; in English, these words are nouns. Supply the appropriate word from the list below.

	Latin Word	Translation	English Meaning
1.	_____	I believe	a statement of belief
2.	_____	I shall please	innocuous medication
3.	_____	remember	souvenir
4.	_____	let it be done	authoritative decree
5.	_____	it is wanting	a shortage
6.	_____	he/she holds	a principle held as true
7.	_____	there is lacking	a proofreading symbol
8.	_____	he/she has sworn	written declaration made under oath
9.	_____	let him/her beware	a warning
10.	_____	we do not know	an uninformed person

affidavit	deficit	lavabo
caret	fiat	memento
caveat	ignoramus	placebo
credo	imprimatur	tenet

4. Match each word with the best definition.

_____ 1. quondam		A. judge
_____ 2. requiem		B. former
_____ 3. quasi		C. a likeness
_____ 4. odium		D. panacea
_____ 5. ergo		E. hatred
_____ 6. simulacrum		F. a very poor person
_____ 7. consortium		G. dirge
_____ 8. nostrum		H. therefore
_____ 9. arbiter		I. resembling
_____10. pauper		J. a large financial partnership

5. Words of Interest. Supply the appropriate word from the list below.

	Latin Word	Translation	English Meaning
1.	_____	shepherd	clergyman
2.	_____	on the left side	ominous; malevolent
3.	_____	sandy place	area used for spectator sports
4.	_____	hearth	center of attention
5.	_____	manly woman	strong woman; shrew
6.	_____	almost-island	Florida, for example
7.	_____	little rod	rod-shaped bacterium
8.	_____	do everything	person employed to do many different things
9.	_____	madness	infectious disease that affects the nervous system
10.	_____	a yawning	a gap; a lapse
11.	_____	threads of life spun by the Fates	endurance
12.	_____	Our Father	Lord's Prayer
13.	_____	make similar	exact copy; fax
14.	_____	mask; character	the character one assumes
15.	_____	spark	trace

arena	hiatus	rabies
bacillus	pastor	scintilla
facsimile	Paternoster	sinister
factotum	peninsula	stamina
focus	persona	virago

6. Expressions of Interest. Supply the appropriate phrase from the list below.

	Latin Word	Translation	English Meaning
1.	_____	in good faith	genuine; sincere
2.	_____	rare bird	unusual person
3.	_____	body of the crime	physical evidence of a crime
4.	_____	another "I"	a second self
5.	_____	into the middle of things	in the middle of a narrative
6.	_____	in glass	in a test tube
7.	_____	one out of many	slogan of the U.S.
8.	_____	my fault	formal acknowledgement of personal fault
9.	_____	in the blazing crime	in the act; red-handed
10.	_____	voice of the people	popular opinion
11.	_____	under the rose	secretly
12.	_____	at one's pleasure	to improvise
13.	_____	not of sound mind	mentally incompetent
14.	_____	nourishing mother	school from which one has graduated
15.	_____	to the man	appealing to emotions rather than intellect

ad hominem	corpus delicti	non compos mentis
ad-lib	e pluribus unum	non sequitur
(ad libitum)	in flagrante delicto	per capita
alma mater	in medias res	rara avis
alter ego	in vitro	sub rosa
bona fide	mea culpa	vox populi

7. Match each phrase with the best definition.

_____	1. status quo	A. something indispensable
_____	2. magnum opus	B. to the point of nausea
_____	3. in situ	C. conversely
_____	4. sine qua non	D. near death
_____	5. pro forma	E. one of a kind; unique
_____	6. sui generis	F. in the original position
_____	7. ad nauseam	G. deductive
_____	8. per se	H. existing state of affairs
_____	9. vice versa	I. carried out as a formality
_____	10. a priori	J. with great distinction
_____	11. in extremis	K. intrinsically
_____	12. ad hoc	L. unwelcome person
_____	13. quid pro quo	M. a great work
_____	14. persona non grata	N. for a particular purpose
_____	15. magna cum laude	O. something given or taken for something else

8. Give the meaning of each of the following Latin abbreviations. The Latin word or phrase is given in parentheses.

1. A.D. (*anno Domini*) *"in the year of our Lord"; a method of dating using the birth of Christ as a starting point*

2. a.m. (*ante meridiem*)

3. c. (*circa*)

4. cf. (*confer*)

5. e.g. (*exempli gratia*)

6. et al. (*et alii*)

7. etc. (*et cetera*)

8. i.e. (*id est*)

9. ibid. (*ibidem*)

10. loc. cit. (*loco citato*)

11. N.B. (*nota bene*)

12. op. cit. (*opere citato*)

13. Q.E.D. (*quod erat demonstrandum*)

14. seq. (*sequente*)

15. vs. (*versus*)

REVIEW OF LESSONS XX–XXV (SELF-TESTING: Answers can be found in Appendix C.)

1. Give the unshortened form of each clipped word.

1. ad _____   4. fan _____
2. auto _____   5. sport _____
3. blitz _____   6. wig _____

2. Supply the appropriate word from the list below.

1. a list of corrections _____

2. our (home) remedy _____

3. a list of things to be done _____

4. with deference to _____

5. something made like another; a copy _____

6. by way of _____

7. the end _____

8. a biological category _____

9. feeling of hostility _____

10. small, insignificant details _____

11. propriety _____

12. official approval _____

agenda	facsimile	minutiae
animus	finis	nostrum
corrigenda	genus	pace
decorum	imprimatur	via

3. Circle the letter of the word that best fits the definition.

1. to condemn: (A) announce   (B) denounce   (C) renounce

2. to appropriate: (A) abrogate   (B) arrogate   (C) derogate

3. to conduct (oneself): (A) comport   (B) report   (C) support

4. to accelerate: (A) capitulate   (B) precipitate   (C) recapitulate

5. a striving to attain: (A) aspiration   (B) inspiration   (C) transpiration

6. enlightening: (A) constructive (B) destructive   (C) instructive

7. to argue: (A) compute   (B) depute   (C) dispute

8. unjustified: (A) gratuitous   (B) gracious   (C) ingratiating

4. Supply the missing base.

1. deathless   im _ _ _ _ al

2. a critical hearing   _ _ _ ition

3. thankfulness   _ _ _ _ itude

4. a seeking   _ _ _ ition

5. to root out   e _ _ _ _ _ ate

6. heartfelt; gracious   _ _ _ _ ial

7. to place   _ _ _ ate

8. height   _ _ _ itude

9. by hand   _ _ _ _ al

10. to behead   de _ _ _ _ _ ate

11. to bend   f _ _ _

12. to sweat   per _ _ _ _ e

13. to invest [a human form] with flesh   in _ _ _ _ ate

14. lack of knowledge   i _ _ _ rance

15. one who conquers   _ _ _ _ or

16. cinema   _ _ _ ies

17. concerning nutrition   _ _ imentary

18. to make common knowledge   di _ _ _ _ e

19. one who fights with the fists   _ _ _ ilist

20. to supply with enough   _ _ _ iate

5. Indicate whether each statement is true or false by circling T or F.

T   F   1. A product bearing the notice *caveat emptor* is likely to be endorsed by a consumer group.

T   F   2. *Loco* (crazy) derives from the base LOC-.

T   F   3. People with an extraordinarily inflated opinion of themselves are said to have an *alter ego.*

T   F   4. If a criminal is caught *in flagrante delicto*, chances are "the jig is up."

T   F   5. The expression "if you scratch my back, I'll scratch yours" is roughly equivalent to the Latin *quid pro quo.*

T   F   6. A defendant's plea of *nolo contendere* in a criminal proceeding is equivalent to an admission of guilt.

T   F   7. Originally, *quaint* meant "knowledgeable" or "clever."

T   F   8. *Brunch* is a blend of the words *breakfast* and *lunch.*

T   F   9. The words *sad* and *sadist* are etymologically related.

T   F   10. In a story beginning *in medias res*, the author starts the narrative in the middle of the sequence of events.

T   F   11. A detective may use the abbreviation *M.O.* to refer to a *modus operandi* of a criminal.

T   F   12. The nouns *chattel* and *capital* form a doublet.

T   F   13. The clipped form of *piano* is "pianoforte."

T   F   14. In a work of literature, a *deus ex machina* appears unexpectedly to resolve a particularly difficult situation.

T   F   15. *Caret* is a Latin word used by jewelers to indicate the weight of precious stones.

6. Match each word with the best definition.

____ 1. destructive	A. a mark made by pressure
____ 2. convict (n.)	B. a severe reproof
____ 3. mixture	C. blend
____ 4. migration	D. a seasonal movement
____ 5. imprint	E. to show clearly
____ 6. purge	F. bellicose
____ 7. proprietor	G. crude
____ 8. moment	H. a person found guilty of committing a crime
____ 9. reprimand	I. to cleanse
____ 10. evince	J. delay
____ 11. terminal (adj.)	K. ruinous
____ 12. pugnacious	L. an instant of time
	M. final
	N. owner

7. Each of the following words has two correct plural forms. Circle the one that is <u>not</u> correct.

1. lacuna: (A) lacunas   (B) lacunae   (C) lacunes

2. matrix: (A) matrixa   (B) matrixes   (C) matrices

3. colloquium: (A) colloquiums   (B) colloquia   (C) colloquiae

4. nucleus: (A) nucleuses   (B) nuclea   (C) nuclei

5. appendix: (A) appendixae   (B) appendices   (C) appendixes

8. The French Connection. The words in this exercise have entered English through French. From the list below, supply the base from which each word derives.

1. mischief   _____

2. lieu   _____

3. recount   _____

4. esprit   _____

5. meddle   _____

6. construe   _____

7. haughty   _____

8. obey   _____

9. motif   _____

10. agreeable   _____

11. rapport   _____

12. mortgage   _____

13. courage   _____

14. announcement   _____

15. maneuver   _____

AL-, ALT-	LOC-	NUNCI-
AUD-	MAN(U)-	PORT-
CAPIT-, (CIPIT-)	MISC-, MIXT-	PUT-
CORD-	MORT-	SPIR-
GRAT-	MOV-, MOT-	STRU-, STRUCT-

9. Match each phrase with the best definition.

_____	1. ad hoc	A. the necessary changes having been made
_____	2. cui bono	B. at first sight
_____	3. modus vivendi	C. solid ground
_____	4. mutatis mutandis	D. manner of living
_____	5. non sequitur	E. voice of the people: popular opinion
_____	6. post scriptum	F. it doesn't follow
_____	7. prima facie	G. for whose good; for whose benefit
_____	8. status quo	H. the exiting state of affairs
_____	9. terra firma	I. something written afterwards
_____	10. vox populi	J. for this only

10. Indicate whether the following pairs are synonyms or antonyms by circling S or A.

S	A	1. gratis	-	costly
S	A	2. dictum	-	pronouncement
S	A	3. apex	-	peak
S	A	4. omen	-	portent
S	A	5. acumen	-	dullness
S	A	6. ardor	-	indifference
S	A	7. effluvium	-	miasma
S	A	8. vertigo	-	equilibrium
S	A	9. proviso	-	stipulation
S	A	10. finis	-	commencement

LATIN REVIEW (LESSONS II–XXV) (SELF-TESTING: Answers can be found in Appendix C.)

1. Indicate whether each statement is true or false by circling T or F.

T   F   1. *Dismal* is made up of the prefix dis- and the base MAL-.

T   F   2. The etymological meaning of *satire* is "medley."

T   F   3. The guillotine is a device that effects death by *recapitulation*.

T   F   4. A *sciolist* is "one who knows little," a possessor of superficial knowledge.

T   F   5. *Sui generis* and *rara avis* both can refer to people or things that are unique.

T   F   6. The word "antidisestablishmentarianism" qualifies as *sesquipedalian*.

T   F   7. The etymology of *nuisance* is someone or something "that harms."

T   F   8. A person who dresses *ostentatiously* dresses in an understated fashion.

T   F   9. The etymology of *penultimate* is "nearly last."

T   F   10. In ancient Rome, a *nomenclator* was a slave who accompanied his master in order to tell him the names of people he met when campaigning for office.

T   F   11. *A.D.* and *B.C.* are both Latin abbreviations.

T   F   12. The prefix in- has the same meaning in the words *ingratiate* and *ingrate*.

T   F   13. *Dirigible* derives from the base REG-, (RIG-), RECT-.

T   F   14. The Latin *sinister* and the French *gauche*, words originally referring to the left, have undergone degeneration of meaning.

T   F   15. *Pro forma* and *rubber stamp* are equivalent in meaning.

2. Supply the missing base.

1. pertaining to sight   _ _ _ ual

2. to think   _ _ _ itate

3. underground   sub _ _ _ _ anean

4. to make by hand   manu _ _ _ _ ure

5. to restore to the fatherland   re _ _ _ _ _ ate

6. changeable   _ _ _ able

7. to write carelessly   _ _ _ _ _ ble

8. manifold   _ _ _ _ iple

9. meat eating   _ _ _ _ ivorous

10. thousand-year period   _ _ _ _ ennium

11. incapable of being heard   in _ _ _ ible

12. pertaining to the end   _ _ _ al

13. farewell address   vale _ _ _ _ ion

14. a place   _ _ _ ale

15. between the lines   inter _ _ _ _ ar

3. Circle the letter of the definition that best fits the underscored word(s).

1. a <u>boon</u> companion: (A) lachrymose   (B) faithful   (C) convivial

2. <u>gratuitous</u> violence: (A) unwarranted   (B) graphic   (C) censored

3. a restaurant's <u>ambiance</u>:   (A) cuisine   (B) atmosphere   (C) service

4. <u>conjugal</u> relations: (A) strained   (B) amiable   (C) between husband and wife

5. <u>illegible</u> handwriting: (A) easily deciphered   (B) unreadable   (C) cursive

6. <u>prenatal</u> care: (A) postpartum   (B) before birth   (C) pertaining to delivery

7. an <u>infraction</u> of the rules: (A) violation   (B) exception   (C) a small portion

8. to <u>avail oneself of</u> a service: (A) pay for   (B) reject   (C) make use of

9. <u>abject</u> poverty: (A) moderate   (B) utterly hopeless   (C) abandoned

10. a <u>persistent</u> salesperson: (A) pertinacious   (B) successful   (C) traveling

11. a <u>voluble</u> personality: (A) talkative   (B) explosive   (C) worthy

12. to <u>discount</u> a theory: (A) originate   (B) disregard   (C) discuss

13. a <u>sullen</u> child: (A) undernourished   (B) only   (C) surly

14. <u>extenuating</u> circumstances: (A) mitigating   (B) embarrassing   (C) relaxing

15. a <u>derogatory</u> remark: (A) inquiring   (B) disparaging   (C) complimentary

16. <u>mortal</u> wounds: (A) fatal   (B) traumatic   (C) corporal

17. a <u>prolific</u> writer: (A) published   (B) suffering from writer's block   (C) productive

18. to <u>divulge</u> a secret: (A) embellish   (B) reveal   (C) maintain

19. to <u>flex</u> one's muscles: (A) relax   (B) build   (C) bend

20. <u>constructive</u> criticism: (A) helpful   (B) unsolicited   (C) adverse

21. an <u>expurgated</u> version of a book: (A) unabridged   (B) bowdlerized   (C) condensed

22. a <u>viable</u> alternative: (A) workable   (B) long-lived   (C) preferable

23. the <u>advent</u> of spring: (A) harbinger   (B) end   (C) arrival

24. a <u>compendious</u> comparison: (A) verbose   (B) concise   (C) grotesque

25. a <u>discursive</u> style: (A) digressive   (B) flowing   (C) severe

4. Form the antonym of each word by substituting another prefix. Remember assimilation (see Appendix A).

1. dissonance   _____ sonance

2. increase   _____ crease

3. proponent   _____ ponent

4. encourage   _____ courage

5. deficient   _____ ficient

6. destructive   _____ structive

7. demotion   _____ motion

8. import   _____ port

5. Occupations. Match each word with the base from which it derives.

_____ 1. artisan A. AG-, (IG-), ACT-

_____ 2. infantry (soldier) B. ART-

_____ 3. prosecutor C. CRUC-

_____ 4. actuary D. FA(B)-, FAT-, FESS-, FAM-

_____ 5. announcer E. FER-

_____ 6. crusader F. LOQU-, LOCUT-

_____ 7. obstetrician G. MIS(S)-, MIT(T)-

_____ 8. exterminator H. NOV-

_____ 9. referee I. NUNCI-, [NOUNC-]

_____ 10. ventriloquist J. SEQU-, SECUT-

_____ 11. novelist K. ST(A)-, STIT-, SIST-

_____ 12. emissary L. TERMIN-

6. Use a check to indicate each clipped word.

_____ 1. flu _____ 3. punctilio

_____ 2. motel _____ 4. decaf

Use a check to indicate each pair of doublets.

_____ 1. afflatus-flaunt _____ 3. count-compute

_____ 2. exclude-foreclose _____ 4. flora-fluorite

Use a check to indicate each word that has undergone elevation of meaning.

_____ 1. constable _____ 3. pioneer

_____ 2. amateur _____ 4. nice

Use a check to indicate each word that has undergone degeneration of meaning.

_____ 1. plausible _____ 3. prestige

_____ 2. wench _____ 4. villain

7. Match each word with its <u>etymological</u> meaning.

____ 1. mélange	A. blazing
____ 2. recantation	B. we do not know
____ 3. flagrant	C. a singing back
____ 4. corpuscle	D. nourishing mother
____ 5. ignoramus	E. to kill every tenth man
____ 6. senator	F. elder
____ 7. spectator	G. disguise
____ 8. pomegranate	H. little body
____ 9. expunge	I. a turning as one
____ 10. decimate	J. to mark out with dots
____ 11. ignominious	K. teacher
____ 12. alma mater	L. mixture
____ 13. universe	M. having no name
____ 14. travesty	N. seedy apple
____ 15. doctor	O. one who watches

8. Indicate whether the following pairs are synonyms or antonyms by circling S or A.

S	A	1. acrimonious	-	stinging
S	A	2. animated	-	vivacious
S	A	3. divinity	-	immortal
S	A	4. educated	-	illiterate
S	A	5. affirm	-	deny
S	A	6. affluent	-	penniless
S	A	7. fallacious	-	veracious
S	A	8. gregarious	-	introverted
S	A	9. precarious	-	dangerous
S	A	10. levity	-	gravity
S	A	11. ordinary	-	mediocre
S	A	12. alien	-	extraterrestrial
S	A	13. model	-	pattern
S	A	14. retreat	-	recede
S	A	15. elate	-	enrapture

9. Match each word with the best definition.

_____ 1. appropriateness	A. to perplex
_____ 2. abstruse	B. circumspect
_____ 3. compatible	C. exoneration
_____ 4. probation	D. to plot
_____ 5. torture	E. difficult to understand
_____ 6. extempore	F. the rhythm of sounds or words
_____ 7. confuse	G. request
_____ 8. residence	H. to inflict pain
_____ 9. cadence	I. conditional release
_____ 10. contagious	J. congruent
_____ 11. conspire	K. capable
_____ 12. able	L. suitability
_____ 13. absolution	M. impromptu
_____ 14. discreet	N. infectious
_____ 15. petition	O. domicile

10. Use a check to indicate each word that has been affected by folk etymology.

_____ 1. female _____ 3. crayfish
_____ 2. pencil _____ 4. reindeer

Use a check to indicate each word that forms a blend.

_____ 1. brunch _____ 3. NATO
_____ 2. rebus _____ 4. buzz

Use a check to indicate each word that is a diminutive.

_____ 1. scruple _____ 3. minuet
_____ 2. senile _____ 4. oracle

11. Identify the prefix (if any) and base in each word and give the meaning of each element; then indicate whether the word is a noun, an adjective, or a verb.

MEANINGS

1. ab | und | ant   _from, away_   _wave_   N <u>A</u> V

2. apartment   _____   N A V

3. aquarium   _____   N A V

4. circumference   _____   N A V

5. corrigendum   _____   N A V

6. defamation   _____   N A V

7. effervesce   _____   N A V

8. endurance   _____   N A V

9. executrix   _____   N A V

10. extrasensory   _____   N A V

11. immigrate   _____   N A V

12. latitude   _____   N A V

13. lectern   _____   N A V

14. pertinacious   _____   N A V

15. precursor   _____   N A V

16. rapid   _____   N A V

17. salient   _____   N A V

18. superfluity   _____   N A V

19. turbulent   _____   N A V

20. verify   _____   N A V

PART II

WORD ELEMENTS FROM GREEK

THE GREEK ALPHABET AND OPTIONAL EXERCISES

Form	Name	Transliteration
Α α	alpha	a
Β β	beta	b
Γ γ	gamma	g
Δ δ	delta	d
Ε ε	epsilon	e
Ζ ζ	zeta	z
Η η	eta	e
Θ θ	theta	th
Ι ι	iota	i
Κ κ	kappa	k, c
Λ λ	lambda	l
Μ μ	mu	m
Ν ν	nu	n
Ξ ξ	xi	x
Ο ο	omicron	o
Π π	pi	p
Ρ ρ	rho	r, rh
Σ σ ς	sigma	s
Τ τ	tau	t
Υ υ	upsilon	u, y
Φ φ	phi	ph
Χ χ	chi	ch
Ψ ψ	psi	ps
Ω ω	omega	o

Part II, The Greek Alphabet

1. **Optional Exercise:** The words in this exercise derive from the names of Greek letters. Supply the appropriate word from the list below.

    1. the complete range   _____

    2. a Christian monogram and symbol   _____

    3. a small amount   _____

    4. the beginning   _____

    5. curved like the letter C or S   _____

    6. rhetorical inversion of two parallel structures _____

    7. the end   _____

    8. anything triangular   _____

    9. excessive use of the sound L   _____

   10. letters of a language in their customary order _____

alpha	delta	omega
alphabet	gamut	sigmoid
chiasmus	iota	
Chi-Rho	lambdacism	

2. **Optional Exercise:** Match each Greek word with its English equivalent.

  ____ 1. φιλοσοφία   A. calliope

  ____ 2. θάνατος   B. kinesis

  ____ 3. νέμεσις   C. prolegomenon

  ____ 4. Σειρήν   D. Thanatos

  ____ 5. κίνησις   E. tantalus

  ____ 6. Καλλιόπη   F. philosophy

  ____ 7. Τάνταλος   G. siren

  ____ 8. προλεγόμενον   H. nemesis

LESSONS I & II

1. In the following two exercises, match each word or phrase with the best definition.

_____ 1. amazon	A. extremely fanciful
_____ 2. Procrustean	B. gloomy
_____ 3. chimerical	C. wise counselor
_____ 4. nemesis	D. to tease
_____ 5. stygian	E. very wealthy man
_____ 6. halcyon	F. strong, powerful woman
_____ 7. mentor	G. calm; peaceful
_____ 8. labyrinth	H. retribution; unbeatable opponent
_____ 9. tantalize	I. a long wandering
_____ 10. odyssey	J. point of vulnerability
_____ 11. aegis	K. maze
_____ 12. Achilles' heel	L. effecting conformity by violent means
	M. extremely changeable
	N. protection; sponsorship

_____ 1. laconic	A. permanently threatening danger
_____ 2. sword of Damocles	B. person of discriminating taste, especially in food and wine
_____ 3. philippic	C. person devoted to luxury
_____ 4. Draconian	D. sun worshiper
_____ 5. solecism	E. stinging condemnation
_____ 6. epicure	F. pertaining to a victory won at great cost
_____ 7. cynic	G. person devoted to house pets, especially dogs
_____ 8. sybarite	H. grammatical or social error
_____ 9. ostracism	I. person who believes all human actions are prompted by self-interest
_____ 10. Pyrrhic	J. extremely harsh
	K. concise
	L. exclusion from society

2. Optional Latin Review: Choose the word or phrase from the list below that fits each expression <u>etymologically</u>.

1. "I could simply die"   _____

2. the heart of the matter   _____

3. "Go with God"   _____

4. having the back part in front   _____

5. a spiritual flock   _____

6. "If you scratch my back, I'll scratch yours" _____

7. person with whom you break bread   _____

8. little mouse   _____

9. a going off the furrow   _____

10. "on the dot"   _____

11. person clad in white   _____

12. moonstruck   _____

13. eater of hashish   _____

14. to harrow again   _____

15. "Give someone a hand"   _____

adieu	congregation	muscle
assassin	core	preposterous
candidate	delirium	punctual
commend	lunatic	quid pro quo
companion	mortified	rehearse

LESSON III

In the following three exercises, match each word with the best definition.

1. OD-

____	1. epode	A. exaggerated expression of feeling
____	2. tragedy	B. a singing back: recantation
____	3. monody	C. concert hall
____	4. odeum	D. short lyric poem
____	5. comedy	E. tune; song
____	6. rhapsody	F. goat song: tale of disaster
____	7. parody	G. burlesque imitation
____	8. palinode	H. mirth song: drama with a happy ending
____	9. melody	I. song sung by one voice
____	10. ode	J. song sung after another song: third part of a Greek ode

2. BIBLI-; CRYPT-, CRYPH-; TOM-

____	1. bibliomania	A. typical or ideal example
____	2. bibliotheca	B. smallest part of an element
____	3. Bible	C. secret; obscure
____	4. bibliography	D. any large, scholarly book
____	5. bibliophile	E. of doubtful authorship
____	6. cryptic	F. obsession with collecting books
____	7. grotesque	G. booklover: collector of books
____	8. apocryphal	H. having a secret name
____	9. cryptonymous	I. list of references
____	10. dichotomy	J. excision of a breast
____	11. epitome	K. collection of books
____	12. tome	L. division, especially of two mutually exclusive groups
____	13. mastectomy	M. distorted in appearance
____	14. atom	N. study of insects
____	15. entomology	O. the Good Book

3. <u>CANON-; CYCL-; GLOSS-, GLOT(T)-; ICON-; MIM-; PYR-</u>

____ 1. canonical	A. pertaining to the tongue
____ 2. bicycle	B. study of artistic symbolism
____ 3. cyclone	C. conforming to a general rule
____ 4. encyclopedia	D. heartburn
____ 5. glossal	E. multilingual
____ 6. gloss	F. a work that contains information on all branches of knowledge
____ 7. polyglot	G. an expert on religious representations
____ 8. iconoclast	H. attacker of established beliefs
____ 9. iconology	I. heavens
____ 10. mimic	J. note of explanation
____ 11. pantomime	K. the telling of a story without words
____ 12. pyromaniac	L. violent storm characterized by circular wind motion
____ 13. pyrosis	M. involving volcanic action
____ 14. empyrean	N. to imitate
____ 15. pyroclastic	O. two-wheeler
	P. pertaining to fire fighting
	Q. person with a passion for setting fires

4. Review: Greek Mythology, History, and Philosophy. Supply the appropriate word from the list below.

1. Race of female warriors   _____

2. Beautiful youth who fell in love with his own image   _____

3. King who wished that everything he touched would turn to gold   _____

4. Structure built to house the Minotaur   _____

5. Protagonist of a Greek tragedy who killed his father and married his mother   _____

6. Place in Greece proverbial for its pastoral way of life   _____

7. Greeks known for rigid self-discipline   _____

8. Sea nymphs whose enticing songs lured men to their deaths   _____

9. River proverbial for its winding course   _____

10. Tomb of Mausolus   _____

11. Mythical highwayman whose bed was "one size fits all"   _____

12. Codifier of extremely severe laws   _____

13. Monster with the head of a lion, the body of a goat, and the tail of a serpent   _____

14. Shield of Zeus and later Athena   _____

15. Famous Cynic in search of an honest man   _____

aegis	Draco	Narcissus
Amazons	labyrinth	Oedipus
Arcadia	Mausoleum	Procrustes
Chimera	Meander	Sirens
Diogenes	Midas	Spartans

5. Optional Latin Review: Indicate whether the following pairs are synonyms or antonyms by circling S or A.

S	A	1. aberrant	-	deviant
S	A	2. approve	-	sanction
S	A	3. ordinary	-	mediocre
S	A	4. supererogatory	-	necessary
S	A	5. impulse	-	incentive
S	A	6. subjoin	-	append
S	A	7. supposition	-	assumption
S	A	8. indiscreet	-	circumspect
S	A	9. divert	-	distract
S	A	10. aggrieved	-	distressed
S	A	11. animated	-	inert
S	A	12. appropriate	-	arrogate
S	A	13. integrity	-	unity
S	A	14. modern	-	antiquated
S	A	15. reclamation	-	restoration

6. Optional Latin and Greek Review: Match each Greek base with a Latin base similar in meaning.

_____	1. PYR-	A. LIBR-
_____	2. BIBLI-	B. CID-, CIS-
_____	3. OD-	C. SCRIB-, SCRIPT-
_____	4. TOM-	D. CIRC-
_____	5. GLOSS-, GLOT(T)-	E. FLAG(R)-, FLAM(M)-
_____	6. GRAPH-	F. CANT-, (CENT-), [CHANT-]
_____	7. ENTOM-	G. LINGU-
_____	8. CYCL-	H. INSECT-

LESSON IV

1. ALG-

Match each word with the best definition.

____	1. pantalgia	A. headache
____	2. nostalgia	B. pain all over
____	3. cephalalgia	C. sensitivity to pain
____	4. neuralgia	D. foot pain
____	5. podalgia	E. fear of pain
____	6. odontalgia	F. pain-producing
____	7. algesia	G. nerve pain
____	8. algogenic	H. "homesickness": a longing for things past
____	9. analgesic	I. toothache
____	10. algophobia	J. painkiller

2. Identify the prefix and base in each word and then give the meaning of each element.

	PREFIX	BASE
1. amphi | bi | ous	*both, around*	*life*
2. anachronism	_____	_____
3. analyze	_____	_____
4. antipodal	_____	_____
5. apogee	_____	_____
6. apotheosize	_____	_____
7. atrophy	_____	_____
8. catalogue	_____	_____
9. catholic	_____	_____
10. dialysis	_____	_____

3. Indicate whether each statement is true or false by circling T or F.

T   F   1. The word *pandemonium* etymologically corresponds to the modern expression "all hell breaking loose."

T   F   2. An atheist would strongly favor the establishment of a *theocracy*.

T   F   3. A *pyrotechnist* is in particular demand on the Fourth of July.

T   F   4. A *pandemic* disease is confined to a small area.

T   F   5. *Eumenides* (Well-minded Ones) is another name for the Greek Furies.

T   F   6. If someone is *chronically* late, the tardiness is habitual.

T   F   7. A person who has an extreme fear of surgical operations should avoid physicians who are *tomomaniacs*.

T   F   8. A *threnody* is performed on festive occasions.

T   F   9. In Greek mythology, the prophecies of *Cassandra* were always heeded and always came true.

T   F   10. *Panacea* and *nostrum* are synonyms.

T   F   11. *Melodious* and *odious* derive from the same Greek base.

T   F   12. The word *monologue* can be used as a synonym for *soliloquy*.

T   F   13. *Grotto* ultimately derives from the Greek base CRYPT-.

T   F   14. *Apocrypha* are writings of certain authenticity.

T   F   15. According to some etymologists, *crony* (close friend) derives from the Greek base CHRON-.

4. LOG-, [-LOGUE]

Match each word with the best definition.

_____ 1. logical   A. concluding section
_____ 2. analogy   B. excessive wordiness
_____ 3. apology   C. the symbol &, for example
_____ 4. dialogue   D. reasonable
_____ 5. logorrhea   E. uncomplimentary
_____ 6. epilogue   F. a group of three plays or literary works
_____ 7. eulogistic   G. expression of regret
_____ 8. dyslogistic   H. a "gathering up" for comparison
_____ 9. trilogy   I. to converse
_____ 10. logogram   J. flattering

5. <u>BI-; GE-; MNE-; POD-; THE-; TROPH-</u>

Match each word with the best definition.

_____ 1. biotic	A. belief in many gods
_____ 2. biography	B. all the gods of a particular people
_____ 3. geometry	C. passionate (lit., having a god within)
_____ 4. amnesia	D. an official forgetting: a general pardon
_____ 5. amnesty	E. origin of the gods
_____ 6. mnemonics	F. speaker's platform
_____ 7. hypermnesia	G. loss of memory
_____ 8. tripod	H. belief in one God
_____ 9. podium	I. an exceptionally poor memory
_____ 10. atheism	J. branch of science dealing with measurement
_____ 11. monotheism	K. relating to life
_____ 12. theogony	L. art of improving the memory
_____ 13. enthusiastic	M. belief in no gods
_____ 14. pantheon	N. an exceptionally excellent memory
_____ 15. hypertrophy	O. the story of a person's life
	P. excessive growth
	Q. three-legged stool

6. Review: Match each Greek-based word with its Latin-based equivalent.

_____ 1. prologue	A. alimentary
_____ 2. pantophagous	B. annals
_____ 3. anthology	C. contemporaneous
_____ 4. chronicles	D. florilegium
_____ 5. analysis	E. multilingual
_____ 6. eclogue	F. omnivorous
_____ 7. polyglot	G. preface
_____ 8. synchronous	H. resolution
_____ 9. monologue	I. literary selection
_____ 10. trophic	J. soliloquy

7. Optional Latin Review: Circle the letter of the word that best fits the definition.

1. endless:
   - (A) determinant
   - (B) exterminate
   - (C) indeterminate
   - (D) interminable

2. to prove guilty:
   - (A) convict
   - (B) convince
   - (C) evict
   - (D) evince

3. onerous:
   - (A) expressive
   - (B) impressive
   - (C) oppressive
   - (D) repressive

4. to grant:
   - (A) accord
   - (B) concord
   - (C) discord
   - (D) record

5. condemnation:
   - (A) denunciation
   - (B) enunciation
   - (C) pronunciation
   - (D) renunciation

6. objective:
   - (A) dispassionate
   - (B) impassioned
   - (C) impassive
   - (D) passionate

7. anatomy:
   - (A) bisection
   - (B) dissection
   - (C) intersection
   - (D) resection

8. to narrate:
   - (A) account
   - (B) count
   - (C) discount
   - (D) recount

9. to summarize:
   - (A) capitulate
   - (B) decapitate
   - (C) precipitate
   - (D) recapitulate

10. apathy:
    - (A) indifference
    - (B) inference
    - (C) preference
    - (D) sufferance

11. poverty:
    - (A) constitution
    - (B) destitution
    - (C) institution
    - (D) substitution

12. epigraph:
    - (A) ascription
    - (B) inscription
    - (C) prescription
    - (D) subscription

13. to free:
    - (A) intermit
    - (B) manumit
    - (C) remit
    - (D) submit

14. to vanquish:
    - (A) compress
    - (B) depress
    - (C) express
    - (D) suppress

15. immediate:
    - (A) constant
    - (B) distant
    - (C) extant
    - (D) instant

LESSON V

1. Identify the prefix and base in each word and then give the meaning of each element.

	PREFIX	BASE
1. dys | troph | y	*bad, disordered, difficult*	*to nourish*
2. eclogue	_____	_____
3. ectoderm	_____	_____
4. empyreal	_____	_____
5. encyclical	_____	_____
6. endogamy	_____	_____
7. ephemeral	_____	_____
8. epigeous	_____	_____
9. eulogize	_____	_____
10. exodus	_____	_____

2. <u>CENTR-</u>

Match each word with the best definition.

____ 1. concentric	A. regarding one's own group as center
____ 2. eccentric	B. single-centered
____ 3. egocentric	C. regarding the sun as center
____ 4. monocentric	D. off-center: peculiar, odd
____ 5. theocentric	E. regarding mankind as center
____ 6. androcentric	F. having a common center
____ 7. ethnocentric	G. regarding God as center
____ 8. heliocentric	H. regarding the self as center
____ 9. geocentric	I. regarding the earth as center
____ 10. anthropocentric	J. regarding males or masculine interests as center

3. Words of Interest. Supply the appropriate word from the list below.

	Word	Etymological Meaning	Current Meaning
1.	_____	empty tomb	monument for person whose body is buried elsewhere
2.	_____	pillar used by ancient Greeks as a gravestone	inscribed stone slab used for commemorative purposes
3.	_____	person sent out	any person who initiates reform
4.	_____	first combatant	leading character in a literary work
5.	_____	something written on a tomb	inscription on a tomb
6.	_____	easy death	mercy killing
7.	_____	for one day only	short-lived
8.	_____	leader of the people	a person who gains power by playing on people's emotions
9.	_____	a meeting	a church council
10.	_____	messenger	a messenger of God
11.	_____	lacking blood	lacking vigor or creativity
12.	_____	message [= a sending to]	a letter, especially a formal one
13.	_____	contest	dramatic conflict among characters in a literary work
14.	_____	Greek garment	woman's scarf or fur
15.	_____	messenger of good news	a preacher of the gospel

agon	demagogue	evangelist
anemic	democrat	leukemia
angel	ephemeral	protagonist
angelophany	epistle	stele
apostle	epitaph	stole
cenotaph	euthanasia	synod

4. AGON-; ANGEL-; DEM-; HEM(AT)-, HAEM(AT)-; OD-, HOD-; STOL-, STAL-, -STLE; THANAT-, THANAS-

Match each word with the best definition.

_____ 1. antagonize	A. affecting many people
_____ 2. Los Angeles	B. a component of red blood cells
_____ 3. epidemic	C. instrument for measuring distance traveled
_____ 4. endemic	D. interval
_____ 5. hemoglobin	E. native
_____ 6. hemorrhage	F. heavy bleeding
_____ 7. hemophiliac	G. city of angels
_____ 8. odometer	H. waves of contraction in the digestive system
_____ 9. exodus	I. departure of a large number of people
_____ 10. methodical	J. to oppose
_____ 11. period	K. obituary
_____ 12. episode	L. a view of death
_____ 13. epistolary	M. "bleeder"
_____ 14. peristalsis	N. catatonic
_____ 15. thanatopsis	O. of or pertaining to letters
	P. systematic
	Q. event

179

5. <u>GAM-</u>

Supply the appropriate word from the list below.

1. If you hate the thought of marriage, you are a _____.

2. If you marry a person while still legally married to another, you could be charged with _____.

3. If you believe in marrying outside of a specific group, you practice _____.

4. If you marry into an equal or higher social group, you are practicing _____.

5. If you think a person should have one spouse at a time, you believe in _____.

6. If you have several spouses at the same time, you are a _____.

7. If you marry for the third time, you enter into _____.

8. If you marry a second time, that marriage is called _____.

bigamy	exogamy	monogamy
digamy	hypergamy	polygamist
endogamy	misogamist	trigamy

6. Indicate whether each statement is true or false by circling T or F.

T   F   1. *Panache* (verve, style) ultimately derives from the base PAN-.

T   F   2. Someone who faints at the sight of blood is *hemophobic*.

T   F   3. If you practice *allogamy*, you are probably a plant.

T   F   4. In some states homicide is punishable by *electrothanasia*.

T   F   5. *Taffy*, a candy, ultimately derives from the base TAPH-.

T   F   6. An *ephemerid* is an insect that is "short-lived."

T   F   7. William Harvey was a pioneer in the study of *hemodynamics*.

T   F   8. *Iconoclast* entered the English language through the world of art; the word originally referred to a careless sculptor.

T F 9. A census provides the government with *demographic* information.

T F 10. A person suffering from *thanatophobia* should avoid precarious situations.

T F 11. A current meaning of *nemesis* is "retribution."

T F 12. A *Pyrrhic victory* is one in which the conquered succumb as a result of total conflagration.

T F 13. *Polka*, the dance, ultimately derives from the base POLY-.

T F 14. *Pantheon* may refer to a group of luminaries in a particular field.

T F 15. A *monoglot* has facility in several languages.

7. **Review:** Match each word with the best definition.

_____ 1. trophic	A. science of climate and weather
_____ 2. polytheism	B. lingual
_____ 3. asynchronous	C. nutritional
_____ 4. panoply	D. heat-producing
_____ 5. meteorology	E. a complete array
_____ 6. anatomy	F. insensitivity to pain
_____ 7. pyrogenetic	G. a structure covering the glottis during swallowing
_____ 8. epiglottis	H. a subterranean burial chamber
_____ 9. cyclic	I. not occurring at the same time
_____ 10. crypt	J. belief in more than one god
_____ 11. agony	K. recurring regularly in succession
_____ 12. glossal	L. anguish
_____ 13. analgesia	M. science dealing with the structure of organisms
_____ 14. octopus	N. eight-footed mollusk

8. **Optional Greek and Latin Review:** Match each Greek prefix with its Latin equivalent.

   ____ 1. amphi-   A. ante-

   ____ 2. apo-   B. sub-

   ____ 3. en-, em-   C. in-

   ____ 4. hyper-   D. super-

   ____ 5. hypo-   E. ad-

                        F. a-, ab-, abs-

                        G. ambi-

9. **Latin Review:** Circle the letter of the definition that best fits the underscored word.

1. a <u>malicious</u> rumor: (A) false (B) unjustified (C) contrived (D) spiteful

2. <u>explicit</u> instructions: (A) precise (B) unclear (C) confusing (D) elaborate

3. <u>pensive</u> expression: (A) happy (B) angry (C) indifferent (D) thoughtful

4. to <u>exacerbate</u> a situation: (A) improve (B) increase the bitterness of
(C) review (D) dismiss

5. in a <u>desultory</u> manner: (A) lucid (B) random (C) hostile (D) unclear

6. to be forced to <u>recant</u>: (A) pay additional taxes (B) admit guilt
(C) withdraw a former statement (D) repeat a task

7. a <u>flagrant</u> error: (A) undetectable (B) conspicuously bad (C) minor
(D) understandable

8. to <u>renounce</u> the kingship: (A) condemn (B) declare (C) give up (D) accept

9. to come to a <u>consensus</u>: (A) agreement (B) compromise (C) stalemate
(D) parting of the ways

10. a <u>sedentary</u> occupation: characterized by (A) few responsibilities (B) standing
(C) frequent relocations (D) sitting

LESSON VI

1. ONYM-

Match each word with its example.

____	1. acronym	A.	Venus (for love)
____	2. antonym	B.	Mark Twain
____	3. eponym	C.	sow (a pig)–sow (to scatter seed)
____	4. heteronym	D.	buzz or choo-choo
____	5. homonym	E.	heal–health
____	6. metonymy	F.	Johnson
____	7. onomatopoeia	G.	Death Valley
____	8. paronym	H.	NATO
____	9. patronymic	I.	fortitude–strength
____	10. pseudonym	J.	bear (to carry)–bear (an animal)
____	11. synonym	K.	Americus Vespucius
____	12. toponym	L.	day–night

2. Identify the prefix and base in each word and then give the meaning of each element.

	PREFIX	BASE
1. hyperpyrexia	_____	_____
2. hyperemia	_____	_____
3. hypogeal	_____	_____
4. metamorphose	_____	_____
5. metaphor	_____	_____
6. paralyze	_____	_____
7. parody	_____	_____

	PREFIX	BASE
8. period	_____	_____
9. periphery	_____	_____
10. problem	_____	_____
11. prognosticate	_____	_____
12. prologue	_____	_____
13. prosody	_____	_____
14. symbol	_____	_____
15. syntax	_____	_____

3. Indicate whether each statement is true or false by circling T or F.

T   F   1. A common *pachyderm*, among the more exotic elephant, hippopotamus, and rhinoceros, is the domestic bore.

T   F   2. The word *jot* ultimately derives from *iota*, a letter of the Greek alphabet.

T   F   3. *Ball* (a lavish party) and the *ball* in *baseball* both derive from the base BALL-.

T   F   4. *Know* is unrelated to the base GNO(S)-.

T   F   5. *Pyrophoric* material is nonflammable.

T   F   6. The etymological meaning of *devil* is "slanderer."

T   F   7. *Dermatitis* means "inflammation of the skin."

T   F   8. The noun *metamorphosis* literally means "changed form."

T   F   9. The word *paraphernalia* originally referred to the personal belongings of a Greek soldier.

T   F   10. Couples having difficulty choosing a name for their new baby may consult an *onomasticon*.

4. BALL-, BOL-, BLE-

The French Connection. The words in this exercise have entered English through French. They ultimately derive from the Greek base BALL-, BOL-, BLE-. Match each word with the best definition.

_____ 1. ballet   A. simple, often sentimental song

_____ 2. parlor   B. idle talk

_____ 3. ballad   C. conditional release from prison

_____ 4. palaver   D. allegorical story

_____ 5. parliament   E. a room suitable for conversation

_____ 6. parlance   F. discussion; informal conference to discuss peace terms

_____ 7. parable   G. any legislative body

_____ 8. parley   H. manner of speaking

_____ 9. parole   I. a classical dance form

5. Circle the letter of the best definition.

1. homily: (A) grits   (B) sermon   (C) ugly

2. semaphore: (A) a visual signaling   (B) diesel trailer (C) microorganism

3. metabolic: (A) ecstatic   (B) figurative   (C) undergoing change

4. mesomorphic: (A) a muscular physique   (B) a heavy body build (C) a slight physique

5. hyperbolic: (A) fiendish   (B) defeated   (C) exaggerated

6. physiognomy: (A) the face, esp. as an index of character   (B) physical geography (C) system of physical laws

7. dogmatic: (A) canine   (B) tenacious   (C) doctrinaire

8. emblem: (A) representation   (B) profit   (C) secret code

9. gnomic: (A) troll-like   (B) characterized by aphorism   (C) pertaining to knowledge

10. orthodox: (A) theological   (B) educational   (C) conventional

11. homogeneous: (A) having the same nature   (B) having the same parent   (C) having the same name

12. tactics: (A) diplomacy   (B) science of touch   (C) strategy

13. amphora: (A) a two-handled vase   (B) insignia   (C) entrails

14. morphology: (A) physical fitness   (B) study of structure or form   (C) study of body types

15. anonymous: (A) in complete agreement   (B) lively   (C) of unknown name

16. gnostic: (A) atheistic   (B) knowing   (C) playful

17. taxidermy: (A) a levy on animal pelts   (B) irritation of the skin   (C) the art of stuffing and mounting animals in lifelike form

18. ballistics: (A) science of training professional dancers   (B) study of the motion of projectiles   (C) study of the healthful effects of bathing

19. diabolic: (A) overthrown   (B) devilish   (C) hot as the devil

20. metaphor: (A) a figure of speech   (B) a system of signals   (C) a striking change

6. Review: Literary Terms. Match each word with the best definition.

_____ 1. eclogue

_____ 2. rhapsodist

_____ 3. trilogy

_____ 4. georgic

_____ 5. mimesis

_____ 6. episode

_____ 7. onomatopoeia

_____ 8. protagonist

_____ 9. cycle

_____ 10. symbol

A. formation of words whose sounds suggest the meaning

B. a poem dealing with farming

C. an object that represents something else through association

D. series of three literary works

E. epic singer in ancient Greece

F. leading actor in a drama

G. series of poems dealing with a single theme or hero

H. a section of an ancient Greek tragedy between two choric songs

I. imitation of nature

J. poem in which shepherds converse

7. Review: For each Greek-based word, supply its Latin-based equivalent from the list below.

1. glossal   _____

2. periphery   _____

3. polymorphous   _____

4. anamnesis   _____

5. entomophagous   _____

6. anonymous   _____

7. dogma   _____

8. prognostication   _____

9. palinode   _____

10. onomastic   _____

11. demotic   _____

12. athanasia   _____

13. metamorphose   _____

14. hypogeal   _____

15. synopsis   _____

circumference	insectivorous	prescience
conspectus	lingual	recantation
doctrine	multiform	recollection
immortality	nominal	subterranean
innominate	popular	transform

8. Review: Greek Mythology, History, and Philosophy. Supply the appropriate word or phrase from the list below.

1. dark; gloomy   _____

2. a permanently threatening danger   _____

3. exclusion from a group   _____

4. a collection of maps   _____

5. clever but fallacious reasoning   _____

6. an evil that cannot be removed by one attempt   _____

7. the Fate who assigned one's destiny   _____

8. a small but vulnerable weakness   _____

9. person who doubts the sincerity of human actions   _____

10. a learned society   _____

academy	cynic	sophistry
Achilles' heel	hydra	stygian
atlas	Lachesis	sword of Damocles
Clotho	ostracism	

REVIEW OF LESSONS I–VI (SELF-TESTING: Answers can be found in Appendix C.)

1. Change the prefix to form the <u>antonym</u> of each word. Then supply the meaning of the antonym.

	Antonym	Meaning of Antonym
1. antonym	_____	_____
2. endoderm	_____	_____
3. dysphoria	_____	_____
4. hypertrophy	_____	_____
5. dyslogistic	_____	_____
6. ectomorph	_____	_____
7. hypoglycemia	_____	_____
8. anode	_____	_____
9. eutrophy	_____	_____
10. katabasis	_____	_____

2. Match each prefix with its meaning.

_____ 1. apo-	A. through; across; between
_____ 2. dia-	B. around; near
_____ 3. en-	C. not; without
_____ 4. epi-	D. from; off
_____ 5. para-	E. in; into
_____ 6. peri-	F. both; on both sides of
	G. beside; disordered
	H. upon; to; in addition to

3. Words of Interest. Supply the appropriate word from the list below.

	Word	Etymological Meaning	Current Meaning
1.	_____	foot-trap	gout
2.	_____	a forgetting	a general pardon
3.	_____	a longing for a return home	a longing for things past
4.	_____	the abode of all demons	utter chaos or disorder
5.	_____	things hidden	works of doubtful authorship
6.	_____	a singing back	retraction
7.	_____	a throwing beyond	exaggeration
8.	_____	cure-all	a remedy for all diseases
9.	_____	a piece cut off	a large, learned book
10.	_____	a bride's goods beyond her dowry	personal belongings
11.	_____	breaker of images	person who attacks established beliefs
12.	_____	wicker basket	small container for food items
13.	_____	state of having a god within	intense excitement
14.	_____	goat song	tale of disaster
15.	_____	government by the people	rule by the majority

agnostic	enthusiasm	pandemonium
amnesty	hyperbole	Pandora
apocrypha	iconoclast	paraphernalia
canister	nostalgia	podagra
demagoguery	palinode	tome
democracy	panacea	tragedy

4. Indicate whether the following pairs are synonyms or antonyms by circling S or A.

S	A	1. protean	-	rigid
S	A	2. angelic	-	demonic
S	A	3. agonizing	-	excruciating
S	A	4. chronic	-	acute
S	A	5. labyrinth	-	maze
S	A	6. orthodox	-	unconventional
S	A	7. anemic	-	vigorous
S	A	8. apocryphal	-	genuine
S	A	9. epicure	-	gourmand
S	A	10. gnome	-	aphorism
S	A	11. siren	-	seductive
S	A	12. pandemic	-	universal
S	A	13. laconic	-	pithy
S	A	14. anomaly	-	consistency
S	A	15. cryptic	-	puzzling

5. Indicate whether each statement is true or false by circling T or F.

T　F　1. *Bigamy* and *digamy* are considered synonymous in current usage.

T　F　2. *Prognosticators* put off until tomorrow what they could be doing today.

T　F　3. The word *panic* owes its origin to the Greek god Pan.

T　F　4. *Hype* is a clipped form of *hypodermic*.

T　F　5. *Tax* and *taxi* both derive from the base TACT-, TAX-.

T   F   6. The word *ostracize* owes its origin to the ancient Greek custom of banishing a citizen by popular vote.

T   F   7. The etymological meaning of *grotesque* is "characteristic of a grotto."

T   F   8. *Canapé* ultimately derives from the base CANON-.

T   F   9. The etymological meaning of *anthology* is "a selection of flowers."

T   F   10. *Dogmatic* and *canine* are synonyms.

6. Match each word with the best definition.

_____   1. panorama

_____   2. systole

_____   3. cryptonym

_____   4. bibliotheca

_____   5. diagnose

_____   6. pyre

_____   7. paralysis

_____   8. epitaph

_____   9. Cyclops

_____ 10. epilogue

_____ 11. gloss

_____ 12. mimic (v.)

_____ 13. atrophy

_____ 14. symbiosis

_____ 15. antipodal

A. collection of books

B. a concluding section

C. loss of sensation due to injury or disease

D. to examine for the purpose of determining a disease

E. to imitate

F. comprehensive survey

G. "round-eye"

H. diametrically opposite

I. empty tomb

J. secret name

K. one of the three Fates

L. the living together of two unlike organisms

M. inscription on a tomb

N. a wasting away; degeneration

O. a note of explanation

P. rhythmic contraction of the heart

Q. pile of combustible material for burning a dead body

LESSON VII

1. <u>AESTHE-, ESTHE-; ANTHROP-; ARCHA(E)-, ARCHE-; GEN(E)-; GER(ONT)-; HOL-; PEP(T)-</u>

Match each word with the best definition.

____	1. esthesis	A. pertaining to old age
____	2. telesthesia	B. mental telepathy
____	3. anthropocentric	C. Gabriel, for example
____	4. archetype	D. sensation
____	5. archangel	E. gloomy
____	6. archipelago	F. of uniform composition
____	7. archenemy	G. origin
____	8. genesis	H. optimistic
____	9. homogeneous	I. original model
____	10. gene	J. creation of the universe
____	11. cosmogony	K. universal
____	12. gerontic	L. insensitivity
____	13. catholic	M. chief foe
____	14. holograph	N. transmitter of hereditary character
____	15. eupeptic	O. expanse of water with many scattered islands
		P. document wholly in the handwriting of its author
		Q. interpreting the world in terms of human experience

2. Indicate whether each statement is true or false by circling T or F.

T F 1. *Proboscis*, an uncomplimentary synonym for "nose," etymologically means "feeder."

T F 2. *Holistic* means "emphasizing the organic unity of the whole."

T F 3. The gods of the ancient Romans and Greeks were not *anthropomorphized*.

T F 4. Ebenezer Scrooge, in Dickens' *A Christmas Carol*, is a classic example of a *misanthrope*.

T	F	5.	Primitive peoples who eat human flesh practice *anthropophagy*.
T	F	6.	The Greek *astral* and the Latinate *stellar* are synonyms.
T	F	7.	The base in *anachronistic* derives from the Greek word for "color," CHROM(AT)-.
T	F	8.	Words like "moo" and "bleat" are *onomatopoeic*.
T	F	9.	*Pediatricians* specialize in treating disorders of the feet.
T	F	10.	The *aster* derives its name from its star-shaped flowers.

3. Words of Interest. Supply the appropriate word from the list below.

	Word	Etymological Meaning	Current Meaning
1.	_____	lover of mankind	humanitarian
2.	_____	star sailor	a person trained for space flight
3.	_____	something old-fashioned	use of an outmoded expression or style
4.	_____	perceiver	a person who is highly sensitive to the beautiful
5.	_____	unfavorable aspect of a star	calamity
6.	_____	chief builder	a person who designs buildings
7.	_____	pertaining to poor digestion	gloomy; irritable
8.	_____	burned whole	complete devastation
9.	_____	little star	a star (*) used as a reference mark
10.	_____	mind doctor	M.D. who specializes in mental disorders

aesthete	asterisk	dyspeptic
archaism	astronaut	holocaust
architect	athlete	philanthropist
archives	disaster	psychiatrist

4. Review: Supply the missing prefix or base.

1. belief in no gods a _ _ _ ism
2. mercy death eu _ _ _ _ _ _ ia
3. a second marriage di _ _ _ y
4. occurring at the same time _ _ _ chronous
5. formless _ morphous
6. empty tomb ceno _ _ _ _
7. excessive growth _ _ _ _ _ trophy
8. a singing back: recantation palin _ _ e
9. booklover _ _ _ _ _ ophile
10. affecting all people pan _ _ _ ic
11. loss of memory a _ _ _ sia
12. self-centered ego _ _ _ _ _ ic
13. having a secret name _ _ _ _ _ onymous
14. devilish dia _ _ _ ical
15. to transform _ _ _ _ morphose
16. story of a person's life _ _ ography
17. place-name top _ _ _ _
18. foot doctor pod _ _ _ _ ist
19. hater of mankind mis _ _ _ _ _ _ _ e
20. pertaining to good digestion eu _ _ _ _ ic

5. Review: Supply the appropriate word from the list below.

WHICH SPECIALIST ARE YOU LIKELY TO CONSULT . . .

1. if you have skin problems?   _____

2. if you are interested in the influence of the
   stars on your future?   _____

3. if you are troubled concerning matters of the soul?   _____

4. if you are interested in the origin and development
   of your own species?   _____

5. if you need your corns removed?   _____

6. if you are experiencing problems associated
   with old age?   _____

7. if you find a cache of arrowheads on your property?   _____

8. if you need advice on the care and feeding
   of your honey bees?   _____

9. if you discover natural gas on your property?   _____

10. if you are designing your own home?   _____

11. if you are tracing your family's pedigree?   _____

12. if you want the head of a male deer
    preserved by having it stuffed and mounted?   _____

13. if you want to buy a rare book?   _____

14. if you need to know the true meaning of a word?   _____

15. if your teeth need straightening?   _____

anthropologist	dermatologist	gerontologist
archaeologist	entomologist	orthodontist
architect	etymologist	podiatrist
astrologer	genealogist	taxidermist
bibliopole	geologist	theologian

6. Optional Latin Review: Match each word with its <u>etymological</u> meaning.

_____ 1. sacrosanct

_____ 2. Occident

_____ 3. pioneer

A. rising [sun]

B. foot soldier

C. doubly holy

D. setting [sun]

E. pilgrim

_____ 4. egregious

_____ 5. crucial

_____ 6. perpetrate

A. to father [a deed]

B. crossroads

C. out from the herd

D. to last indefinitely

E. pertaining to a ruler

_____ 7. vulgar

_____ 8. ignominious

_____ 9. senescent

A. unkempt

B. aging

C. having no name

D. having Alzheimer's disease

E. common

_____ 10. nasturtium

_____ 11. nice

_____ 12. infant

A. ignorant

B. nose-twister

C. one who cannot speak

D. pleasant

E. stinking flower

_____ 13. stable

_____ 14. effervescent

_____ 15. cursory

A. running

B. small standing place [for animals]

C. in due course

D. bubbly

E. animal fur

7. Optional Greek Review: Select the appropriate mythological figure(s) from the list below.

1. Sylvan deity with cloven hoof   _____

2. Visage that launched a thousand ships   _____

3. Supreme ruler of the ancient Greek gods   _____

4. Aliferous steed   _____

5. A hero of the Trojan War with a bad case
   of homesickness   _____

6. Hero who performed twelve different feats   _____

7. Goddess born by cephalectomy   _____

8. Hippanthropic creature   _____

9. One look is all it took to be petrified by her   _____

10. Canine guard of the gates of hell   _____

11. Woman who, outraged by her husband's
    abandonment, commits filicide   _____

12. Hero with a vulnerable sole   _____

Achilles	Helen	Odysseus
Athena	Hercules	Pan
Centaur	Medea	Pegasus
Cerberus	Medusa	Zeus

LESSON VIII

1. CHROM(AT)-; CRI-; ETHN-; PHA(N)-

Match each word with the best definition.

____	1. chromatic	A. a review
____	2. criterion	B. relating to races
____	3. critique	C. to express forcefully
____	4. oneirocritic	D. pertaining to color
____	5. ethnology	E. cultural anthropology
____	6. ethnic	F. a standard
____	7. theophany	G. an observable circumstance
____	8. emphasize	H. servile flatterer
____	9. sycophant	I. visible appearance of a deity
____	10. phenomenon	J. dream interpreter

2. PHIL-; PHON-; POLY-; THERM-

Match each word with the best definition.

____	1. philter	A. booklet
____	2. pamphlet	B. caused by heat
____	3. megaphone	C. belief in many gods
____	4. stereophonic	D. instrument that measures temperature
____	5. symphonic	E. harmonious
____	6. polygon	F. state of having more than one wife at the same time
____	7. polygyny	
____	8. polytheism	G. love potion
____	9. thermometer	H. a many-sided figure
____	10. thermal	I. producing the effect of three-dimensional sound
		J. a cone-shaped instrument that magnifies the voice

3. Words of Interest. Supply the appropriate word from the list below.

	Word	Etymological Meaning	Current Meaning
1.	_____	stage actor	dissembler
2.	_____	showing through	very sheer
3.	_____	decision	a decisive or crucial moment
4.	_____	the saying of the same things	needless repetition
5.	_____	[literary] selection	a pastoral poem
6.	_____	a sound in response	a song of praise; hymn
7.	_____	appearance	imagination; daydream
8.	_____	an instrument that records many things	lie detector
9.	_____	lover of lights	matchbook collector
10.	_____	a gathering up	miscellanea of selected literary passages

analects	eclogue	polygraph
anthem	fantasy	polyptych
crisis	hypocrite	sycophant
diaphanous	phillumenist	tautology

4. Indicate whether each statement is true or false by circling T or F.

T F 1. *Lexicographers* write dictionaries.

T F 2. *Philippa* (PHIL- + [H]IPP-) is an appropriate name for an equestrienne.

T F 3. *Phony* derives from the base PHON-.

T F 4. The word *polymath* refers to an exceptionally gifted mathematician.

T F 5. A person suffering from *achromatopsia* is color-blind.

T   F   6. *Philately* is an example of an avocation.

T   F   7. *Phantasmagoria* may refer to a scene composed of many images.

T   F   8. *Criticaster* is another name for a movie reviewer on radio or television.

T   F   9. *Ciao* is an Italian loan word.

T   F   10. Americans who travel in Europe and assume that everyone speaks English reveal their *ethnocentricity*.

5. Review: Words with Religious Associations. Match each word with the base from which it derives.

_____ 1. apostle	A. ANGEL-	
_____ 2. evangelist	B. BALL-, BOL-, BLE-	
_____ 3. apocrypha	C. BIBLI-	
_____ 4. Bible	D. CANON-	
_____ 5. epiphany	E. CRYPT-, CRYPH-	
_____ 6. holocaust	F. CYCL-	
_____ 7. agnostic	G. D(A)EMON-	
_____ 8. parable	H. DOX-, DOG-	
_____ 9. canons	I. GNO(S)-	
_____ 10. encyclical	J. HOL-	
_____ 11. psalmody	K. HOM(E)-	
_____ 12. orthodox	L. OD-	
_____ 13. demonic	M. OD-, HOD-	
_____ 14. exodus	N. PHA(N)-	
_____ 15. homily	O. STOL-, STAL-, -STLE	

6. Review: Supply the missing prefix or base.

1. with feet opposite   anti _ _ _ al

2. capable of life on both land and water   _ _ _ _ _ bious

3. having many centers   poly _ _ _ _ _ ic

4. without nourishment   _ trophic

5. person with a passion for setting fires   _ _ _ omaniac

6. something back in (or out of) time   _ _ _ chronistic

7. speaking one language   mono _ _ _ _

8. to imitate   _ _ _ ic

7. Optional Latin Review: Food and Drink. Match each word with the base from which it derives.

____ 1. minestrone	A. AC(U)-, ACR-, ACET-
____ 2. cabbage	B. CAPIT-, (CIPIT-)
____ 3. preserves	C. COR-
____ 4. parfait	D. DE-, DIV-
____ 5. pomegranate	E. FAC-, (FIC-), FACT-, (FECT-)
____ 6. passion fruit	F. FUND-, FUS-, [FOUND-]
____ 7. fondue	G. GRAN-
____ 8. purée	H. MINOR-, MINUS-, MINUT-
____ 9. horseradish	I. PATI-, PASS-
____ 10. divinity (fudge)	J. PORT-
____ 11. cordial	K. PURG-
____ 12. salsa	L. RADIC-
____ 13. port	M. SAL- (salt)
____ 14. torte	N. SERV-
____ 15. vinaigrette	O. TORT-

LESSON IX

1. <u>POL-, -POLIS</u>

Match each word with the best definition.

____ 1. acropolis		A. city-state
____ 2. Annapolis		B. miniature city
____ 3. cosmopolis		C. large city
____ 4. metropolis		D. "new city"
____ 5. Tripoli		E. the fortified upper part of an ancient Greek city
____ 6. necropolis		F. "Queen Anne's city"
____ 7. polis		G. ghost town
____ 8. Naples		H. "city of the dead"
		I. city of worldwide importance
		J. "triple city"

2. Indicate whether each statement is true or false by circling T or F.

T   F   1. The etymological meaning of *cosmetics* is "substances intended to bring order."

T   F   2. A person suffering from *pedantry* should consult a *podiatrist*.

T   F   3. A *heterodoxical* view is in accordance with standard doctrines.

T   F   4. *Polyp* and *polio* belong to the same family of words.

T   F   5. *Neologism* refers to the use or coinage of new words.

T   F   6. The prehistoric *mastodon* derives its name from the breast-shaped projections on its molars.

T   F   7. The majority of states in the U.S. have Native American names.

T   F   8. Cologne, Germany, derives its name from *Colonia Agrippina*, an early Roman colony.

T   F   9. *Nevada* ultimately derives from the Latin for "salty"; the state owes its name to its capital city.

T   F   10. Sir Water Raleigh named one of the thirteen colonies *Virginia* because it was "unspoiled land."

3. Words of Interest. Supply the appropriate word from the list below.

	Word	Etymological Meaning	Current Meaning
1.	_____	a slave who led a child to and from school	teacher
2.	_____	well-rounded or general education	a work covering all branches of knowledge
3.	_____	generalship	military tactics
4.	_____	correct writing	spelling
5.	_____	person who works with the hands	a physician who treats diseases by operation
6.	_____	divination by studying the hands	palmistry
7.	_____	a seeing together	a short summary
8.	_____	a looking with one's own eyes	postmortem examination
9.	_____	new (element)	a gaseous element used for illuminating signs
10.	_____	of another land	foreign
11.	_____	citizenship	a particular system of government
12.	_____	a little something in the hand	handbook

autopsy	heterochthonous	police
calligraphy	neon	polity
chiromancy	orthography	strategy
enchiridion	pedagogue	surgeon
encyclopedia	pederast	synopsis

4. **Optional Latin and Greek Review:** Place Names. Using your knowledge of Latin and Greek elements, match each toponym with its <u>etymological</u> meaning.

____ 1. Chersonese	A. clear water
____ 2. Florence	B. new Scotland
____ 3. Eau Claire	C. brotherly love
____ 4. Vera Cruz	D. dry island
____ 5. Thermopylae	E. prosperous
____ 6. Nova Scotia	F. encircling
____ 7. Tierra del Fuego	G. true cross
____ 8. Corpus Christi	H. warm gates
____ 9. Philadelphia	I. body of Christ
____ 10. Cyclades	J. land of fire

5. **Review:** Circle the letter of the best definition.

1. thermal: (A) a vacuum bottle   (B) pertaining to heat   (C) having to do with long underwear

2. phonetic: (A) frenzied   (B) serving to amplify sound   (C) pertaining to speech sounds

3. philately: (A) generosity   (B) a series of love affairs   (C) stamp collecting

4. tautology: (A) needless repetition   (B) entirety   (C) study of similar expression

5. phantasmagoria: (A) a series of constantly shifting scenes   (B) spiritualism (C) extraordinarily good fortune

6. lexicon: (A) a book of laws   (B) dictionary   (C) a flexible plastic

7. chromosome: (A) pigment-producing cell   (B) a colorful body (C) one of the bodies in a cell nucleus that carries genetic material

8. criticaster: (A) a television movie reviewer   (B) one who finds fault (C) an inferior critic

9. ethnology: (A) a study of animal behavior   (B) cultural anthropology (C) study of moral values

10. pepsin: (A) an enzyme secreted by the stomach   (B) a cure for indigestion (C) a soft drink

11. holistic: (A) sacred   (B) emphasizing the organic unity of the whole
    (C) having a depression or concavity

12. epigone: (A) an angled figure   (B) an inferior imitator   (C) embodiment

13. astrolabe: (A) stargazer   (B) the degree of brightness of a star
    (C) an instrument used by the ancient Greeks to determine the position of
    stars

14. archangel: (A) eldest angel   (B) chief angel   (C) youngest angel

15. embolism: (A) destructive metabolism   (B) occlusion of a blood vessel
    (C) physiological processes of an organism

16. aesthete: (A) competitor   (B) person of the highest class
    (C) one who affects sensitivity to the beautiful

17. syntax: (A) an additional tax   (B) strategy   (C) grammar

18. amorphous: (A) loving   (B) lacking definite form   (C) shapely

19. anomaly: (A) an assumed name   (B) a marine animal with tentacles
    (C) abnormality

20. prognosis: (A) determination of the identity of an illness   (B) forecast
    (C) predestination

LESSON X

1. Identify the prefix (if any) and base(s) in each word and then give the meaning of each element.

MEANINGS OF PREFIXES, BASES

1. amnesia _____

2. cacophony _____

3. cosmopolite _____

4. enthusiast _____

5. iconoclast _____

6. neologism _____

7. neophyte _____

8. optician _____

9. orthodontist _____

10. prophet _____
(See Lesson XI)

2. <u>PATH-</u>

Match each word with the best definition.

_____ 1. antipathy   A. poignancy
_____ 2. pathological   B. lack of feeling
_____ 3. empathy   C. a strong feeling of aversion
_____ 4. pathos   D. compassionate
_____ 5. sympathetic   E. caused by disease
_____ 6. apathy   F. vicarious experiencing of the feeling of others

3. Words of Interest. Supply the appropriate word from the list below.

	Word	Etymological Meaning	Current Meaning
1.	_____	forgetful and lazy	sluggish
2.	_____	work	unit of work [in physics]
3.	_____	treasure	dictionary of synonyms and antonyms
4.	_____	something put in beside something else	pair of signs ( ) used to indicate an aside
5.	_____	a thing devoted (to evil)	a curse; object of loathing
6.	_____	storehouse	pharmacy
7.	_____	something burned in	fluid used for writing
8.	_____	perception from afar	extrasensory communication
9.	_____	the act of speaking otherwise	symbolic narrative
10.	_____	burning heat [of midday]	tranquility; serenity
11.	_____	bad character	mania
12.	_____	a standing out from oneself; derangement	rapture
13.	_____	an unpublished story	telling of a short, amusing incident
14.	_____	to brand	to burn with fire for curative purposes
15.	_____	something given against	medicine to counteract the effects of poison

allegory   calm   hypothesis
anathema   cauterize   ink
anecdote   dynamite   lethargic
antidote   dynasty   parenthesis
apothecary   ecstasy   telepathy
cacoëthes   erg   thesaurus

4. <u>ALL-; CAC-; CAU(S)-; DO-; DYN(AM)-; ERG-, URG-; PHY-; PHYSI-; STA-; THE-</u>

Match each word with the best definition.

____ 1. parallel	A.	a body of rites
____ 2. cacology	B.	corrosive; biting
____ 3. caustic	C.	measured quantity of a drug
____ 4. holocaust	D.	sports arena
____ 5. dose	E.	body build
____ 6. dynasty	F.	a powerful family
____ 7. dynamo	G.	opposition
____ 8. liturgy	H.	complete destruction
____ 9. physique	I.	a proposal set forth for consideration
____ 10. metaphysical	J.	deserter of a cause or religion
____ 11. stadium	K.	producing an effect
____ 12. apostate	L.	conjectural
____ 13. hypothetical	M.	mispronunciation
____ 14. antithesis	N.	analogous
____ 15. thesis	O.	calisthenics
	P.	an energetic person
	Q.	supernatural; abstruse

5. Indicate whether each statement is true or false by circling T or F.

T   F   1. *Dossier* ultimately derives from the Greek base DO-.

T   F   2. The name *Theodore* means "gift of God."

T   F   3. "May he/she rest in peace" is an *epithet* once commonly inscribed on tombs.

T   F   4. *Cacography* can refer to incorrect spelling or illegible handwriting.

T   F   5. A *red-letter day* originally signified a holy day.

T   F   6. Medical examiners are specialists in *pathology*.

T   F   7. The frequently heard pronunciation of "athlete" as three syllables (ath-a-lete) illustrates the linguistic phenomenon of *epenthesis*.

T   F   8. *Diacritical* marks do not facilitate pronunciation by "distinguishing between" sounds.

T   F   9. The ancient Druids practiced *dendrolatry*.

T   F   10. The word *doll* probably originated as a nickname for "Dorothy."

6. For further practice using familiar and unfamiliar Greek bases, supply the appropriate word from the lists below in the following two exercises.

PHIL-

1. a connoisseur of wine   _____

2. affection for mankind   _____

3. thriving in strong light   _____

4. a lover of France or the French   _____

5. a lover of learning and literature   _____

6. a bacterium that grows best in warm temperatures   _____

7. having an affinity for animals   _____

8. fond of music   _____

9. a friend or supporter of the Greeks   _____

10. a booklover   _____

11. a tree-loving plant   _____

12. a connoisseur of high-fidelity sound reproduction   _____

13. having a strong affinity for water   _____

14. a tendency to bleed profusely   _____

15. a lover of England or the English   _____

Anglophile	hydrophilic (XIII)	philodendron (XXV)
audiophile	oenophile	philologist
bibliophile	philanthropy	photophilous (XIV)
Francophile	philharmonic	thermophile
hemophilia	philhellene	zoophilous (XIII)

LAT(E)R-

Worship of . . .

1. idols   _____

2. work   _____

3. books   _____

4. evil spirits   _____

5. icons   _____

6. fire   _____

7. the dead   _____

8. the sun   _____

9. animals   _____

10. a deity   _____

bibliolatry	iconolatry	theolatry
demonolatry	idolatry	zoolatry (XIII)
ergolatry	necrolatry (XII)	
heliolatry	pyrolatry	

7. **Review:** For each Greek-based word, supply the appropriate Latinate synonym from the list below.

1. myth   _____

2. mimic   _____

3. apotheosis   _____

4. comedian   _____

5. enchiridion   _____

6. dialogue   _____

7. chaos   _____

8. neophyte   _____

9. diaphanous   _____

10. antagonist   _____

11. anathema   _____

12. endogenous   _____

13. analogous   _____

14. epistle   _____

15. cosmos   _____

adversary	imitate	native
confusion	legend	novice
conversation	malediction	similar
deification	manual	transparent
humorist	missive	universe

LESSON XI

1. <u>KINE-, CINE-; GYN(E)-, GYN(A)EC-; LITH-, LITE-; MIS-; PHE(M)-, PHA-;
SCHIZ-, SCHIS-; STERE-; TYP-</u>

   Match each word with the best definition.

____ 1. kinetic	A. loss of speech
____ 2. cineast	B. division
____ 3. psychokinesis	C. woman hater
____ 4. misogynist	D. caused by motion
____ 5. monolith	E. a single, massive block of stone
____ 6. lithography	F. picture tube
____ 7. blame (n.)	G. culpability
____ 8. aphasia	H. unusual
____ 9. blaspheme	I. devotee of movies
____ 10. prophet	J. producing a three-dimensional effect of sound
____ 11. euphemism	K. to revile
____ 12. schism	L. lumber
____ 13. stereophonic	M. original model
____ 14. archetype	N. a printing process using metal plates
____ 15. atypical	O. mind controlling matter
	P. substitution of an innocuous expression for an offensive one
	Q. person who speaks for God

2. Indicate whether each statement is true of false by circling T or F.

   T   F   1. *Idiot* originally referred to a private person who chose to refrain from public office.

   T   F   2. Originally, the verb *orient* meant to situate a church in the proper position, with its altar at the east end.

   T   F   3. If someone has ingested poison, an *anecdote* must be administered immediately.

   T   F   4. The etymological meaning of *idiosyncrasy* is "one's own private mixture."

T   F   5. Originally, a *gossip* was a godparent.

T   F   6. People who say that certain activities are "women's work" or "men's work" are perpetuating a *stereotype*.

T   F   7. A *misologist* dislikes discord of any kind.

T   F   8. Men who put women on lofty pedestals might be described as *gyneolatrous*.

T   F   9. Originally, a *bonfire* was for burning bones.

T   F   10. *Chartreuse* is the name of a color, a yellow-green liqueur, and a monastery near Grenoble, France.

T   F   11. *Pantheon* and *apothecary* belong to the same family of words.

T   F   12. The great majority of words with Greek origins have been formed in modern times.

3. Review: For each Greek-based word, supply its Latin-based equivalent from the list below.

 1. dynast   _____

 2. gerontic   _____

 3. prophecy   _____

 4. metathesis   _____

 5. cinema   _____

 6. demos   _____

 7. prolepsis   _____

 8. symphonic   _____

 9. hypothesis   _____

10. eclectic   _____

11. prognosticative   _____

12. sympathy   _____

13. antithetical   _____

14. polychromatic   _____

15. lexicon   _____

anticipation	multicolored	prescient
compassion	opposite	selective
consonant	populace	senescent
dictionary	potentate	supposition
movies	prediction	transposition

4. **Review:** Match each word with the best definition.

____ 1. cosmopolite   A. empty tomb

____ 2. epiphany   B. conforming to usual beliefs

____ 3. cenotaph   C. a combining into a single entity

____ 4. mimesis   D. comprehensive presentation

____ 5. Thanatos   E. to execrate

____ 6. chronometer   F. visible appearance of a deity

____ 7. panorama   G. a newborn child

____ 8. homotaxis   H. death personified in Greek myth

____ 9. antagonize   I. inability to read

____ 10. synthesis   J. a "world citizen"

____ 11. orthodox   K. to provoke hostility

____ 12. peripheral   L. imitation

____ 13. anathematize   M. marginal

____ 14. neonate   N. a very accurate timepiece

____ 15. alexia   O. similarity in arrangement

5. Optional Latin Review: Words with Religious Associations. Match each word with the base from which it derives.

_____	1. commandments	A.	CANT-, (CENT-), [CHANT-]
_____	2. reparation	B.	FA(B)-, FAT-, FESS-, FAM-
_____	3. chant	C.	GRAD-, GRESS-
_____	4. congregation	D.	GRAT-
_____	5. service	E.	GREG-
_____	6. transgress	F.	MAN(U)-
_____	7. convert	G.	NOMEN-, NOMIN-
_____	8. grace	H.	NON-
_____	9. Vulgate	I.	PAR-
_____	10. Unitarian	J.	REG-, (RIG-), RECT-
_____	11. noon	K.	SERV-
_____	12. rector	L.	SCRIB-, SCRIPT-
_____	13. confessional	M.	UN-
_____	14. denominational	N.	VERT-, VERS-
_____	15. scripture	O.	VULG-

6. Optional Latin Review: Match each word with its <u>etymological</u> meaning.

_____	1. sonnet	A.	to return to one's fatherland
_____	2. biceps	B.	sated
_____	3. sad	C.	war-waging
_____	4. cull	D.	removal of meat
_____	5. evolve	E.	new growth
_____	6. enchant	F.	to unfold
_____	7. repair	G.	two-headed
_____	8. haughty	H.	runner
_____	9. frail	I.	to cast a spell on
_____	10. belligerent	J.	breakable
_____	11. foreclose	K.	to gather
_____	12. recruit	L.	to shut outside
_____	13. carnival	M.	one who cannot speak
_____	14. corsair	N.	little song
_____	15. infant	O.	high; lofty

Name _____

REVIEW OF LESSONS VII–XI (SELF-TESTING: **Answers can be found in Appendix C.**)

1. Match each word with the best definition.

____	1. genethliac	A. redundant
____	2. phantom	B. vigorous; energetic
____	3. doxology	C. pertaining to birthdays
____	4. tautologous	D. causing disease
____	5. overdose	E. ghost
____	6. allegorical	F. to take an excessive amount of a drug
____	7. pathogenic	G. concerned with the whole
____	8. acrolith	H. figurative
____	9. holistic	I. hymn of praise
____	10. dynamic	J. In Greek sculpture, a statue whose head and extremities only were of stone

2. Supply the missing prefix or base to form the antonym of each word.

1. hyperesthesia   _ _ _ esthesia

2. homogeneous   _ _ _ _ _ ogeneous

3. eupeptic   _ _ _ peptic

4. misanthrope   _ _ _ _ anthropist

5. monogamy   _ _ _ _ gamy

6. heterodox   _ _ _ _ odox

7. antipathy   _ _ _ pathy

8. polygyny   poly _ _ _ _ y

9. euphony   _ _ _ ophony

10. prologue   _ _ _ logue

217

3. Identify the prefix (if any) and base(s) in each word and give the meaning of each element. Then indicate whether the word is a noun or adjective by circling N or A.

	PREFIX	BASE(S)		
1. phonetics	_____	_____	N	A
2. geriatric	_____	_____	N	A
3. technical	_____	_____	N	A
4. hyperkinesis	_____	_____	N	A
5. neophyte	_____	_____	N	A
6. misogynist	_____	_____	N	A
7. hypocrisy	_____	_____	N	A
8. optician	_____	_____	N	A
9. cosmopolite	_____	_____	N	A
10. emblematic	_____	_____	N	A
11. prognosis	_____	_____	N	A
12. anathema	_____	_____	N	A
13. aesthete	_____	_____	N	A
14. astral	_____	_____	N	A
15. euphemism	_____	_____	N	A
16. schizogenic	_____	_____	N	A
17. exodontia	_____	_____	N	A
18. apostate	_____	_____	N	A
19. emphatic	_____	_____	N	A
20. dynast	_____	_____	N	A

4. Match each word with the best definition.

_____ 1. synergy		A. lacking color
_____ 2. stereotyped		B. worship of images
_____ 3. idiocy		C. pertaining to a particular culture
_____ 4. achromatic		D. opposing religion
_____ 5. pedagogy		E. sarcastic
_____ 6. caustic		F. relating to medicine
_____ 7. antithetical		G. art of teaching
_____ 8. iatric		H. teamwork
_____ 9. iconolatry		I. expensive
_____ 10. ethnic		J. extreme stupidity
		K. opposite
		L. conventional

5. Indicate whether each statement is true or false by circling T or F.

T   F   1. The word *pamphlet* originally referred to a humorous, amatory work of the twelfth century.

T   F   2. *Cincinnati* is named after the famous Roman general Marcus Tullius Cicero.

T   F   3. The etymology of *Gallipoli* is "city of the Gauls."

T   F   4. *Good-bye* is a contraction of "God be with you."

T   F   5. *Parliament* belongs to the BALL-, BOL-, BLE- family of words.

T   F   6. In the expression "to eat humble pie," *humble* owes its spelling to folk etymology.

T   F   7. "A stitch in time saves nine" is an example of an *apothegm*.

T   F   8. The word *talent* originally referred to an amount of money.

T   F   9. The expression "flash in the pan" derives from the California gold rush of 1849.

T   F   10. The etymology of *chiropractor* is "one who works with the feet."

LESSON XII

1. <u>AUT-; GASTR-; HELI-; IDE-; MICR-; NECR-; PAL(A)E-; PSEUD-; PSYCH-; TROP-</u>

   Match each word with the best definition.

____ 1. automatic	A. soul or mind
____ 2. gastric	B. plant that turns toward the sun
____ 3. idea	C. mechanical
____ 4. microscopic	D. pertaining to primitive man
____ 5. necrophagous	E. very small
____ 6. paleanthropic	F. gourmet
____ 7. pseudo	G. false; counterfeit
____ 8. psyche	H. pertaining to the stomach
____ 9. apotropaic	I. the act of nurturing by the sun
____ 10. heliotrope	J. notion
	K. feeding on carrion
	L. intended to ward off evil

2. Indicate whether each statement is true or false by circling T or F.

   T   F   1. A person suffering from *necrophobia* is unlikely to pursue a career as a mortician.

   T   F   2. Sunflowers belong to the genus *Helianthus*.

   T   F   3. During the summer months, beaches are filled with present-day *heliolaters*.

   T   F   4. The word *authentic* derives from the bases AUT- + THE-.

   T   F   5. Agricultural students take courses in *agronomy*.

   T   F   6. *Necrology* and *obituary* do not mean the same thing.

   T   F   7. The etymology of *economics* is "household management."

   T   F   8. *Micropaleontology* is the study of large fossils.

   T   F   9. Australian aborigines are *autochthonous* peoples.

   T   F   10. The word *idolater*, besides referring to a worshiper of idols, can pertain to someone who admires an object too intensely.

   T   F   11. Etymologically, *inaugurate* means "to consult the omens" before engaging in an important matter.

   T   F   12. *Pseudonym* and *nom de plume* are synonyms for "pen name."

T   F   13. The etymology of *neophyte* is "new growth."
T   F   14. An expression that is *parenthetical* "adds something beside."
T   F   15. Little Rock, Arkansas, was formerly known as Last Chance Gulch.

3. Words of Interest. Supply the appropriate word from the list below.

1. study of ancient handwriting   _____

2. self-taught   _____

3. gourmet   _____

4. physician who treats the mind   _____

5. self-rule   _____

6. brightly colored   _____

7. elaborate cemetery of an ancient city   _____

8. palmistry   _____

9. "the Unrelenting One": the Greek Fate who
who cut the thread of life   _____

10. abnormal fear of corpses   _____

11. a pastoral composition   _____

12. financial considerations   _____

13. a world in miniature   _____

14. a person sensitive to supernatural forces   _____

15. prophetic   _____

Atropos   gastronome   necropolis
autodidactic   idyll   paleography
autonomy   mantic   psychedelic
chiromancy   microcosm   psychiatrist
economics   necrophobia   psychic

4. Supply the missing base.

1. study of life   _ _ ology

2. study of humankind   _ _ _ _ _ _ _ ology

3. study of the earth   _ _ ology

4. study of God   _ _ _ ology

5. study of the elderly   _ _ _ _ _ _ ology

6. study of the mind   _ _ _ _ _ ology

7. study of the blood   _ _ _ _ _ ology

8. study of family trees   _ _ _ _ alogy

9. study of evil spirits   _ _ _ _ _ ology

10. study of form and structure   _ _ _ _ _ ology

11. study of insects   en _ _ _ ology

12. science that deals with the skin   _ _ _ _ _ _ ology

13. science that deals with the universe   _ _ _ _ ology

14. divination of the supposed influence   _ _ _ _ ology
    of the stars

15. study of cultures   _ _ _ _ ology

5. Supply the appropriate word from the list below.

IF YOU LIVE IN A(N) . . .

1. _____, the majority rules.

2. _____, the mob rules.

3. _____, all rule equally.

4. _____, the best people rule.

5. _____, those divinely guided rule.

6. _____, two regents rule.

7. _____, a few rule.

8. _____, the old rule.

9. _____, women rule.

10. _____, a single regent rules.

11. _____, the father rules.

12. _____, technical experts rule.

13. _____, there is an absence of government.

14. _____, the rich rule.

15. _____, the military rule.

anarchy	gynecocracy	patriarchy
aristocracy	monarchy	plutocracy
democracy	ochlocracy	stratocracy
dyarchy	oligarchy	technocracy
gerontocracy	pantisocracy	theocracy

6. Review: Supply the missing base.

1. pertaining to color	c _ _ _ _ _ _ ic
2. lover of mankind	_ _ _ _ anthropist
3. world citizen	cosmo _ _ _ ite
4. having many forms	_ _ _ _ morphous
5. unit of work	e _ _
6. little star (*)	_ _ _ _ _ isk
7. one who speaks for God	pro _ _ _ t
8. original model	arche _ _ _ e
9. relating to three-dimensional sound	_ _ _ _ _ ophonic
10. the movies	_ _ _ _ ma

7. Optional Latin Review: Words with Religious Associations. Match each word with the base from which it derives.

____ 1. deity		A.	ANIM-
____ 2. animism		B.	CARN-
____ 3. oracle		C.	CRUC-
____ 4. genius		D.	DE-, DIV-
____ 5. immortals		E.	GEN-
____ 6. crucify		F.	MIGR-
____ 7. reincarnation		G.	MORT-
____ 8. prayer		H.	OR-
____ 9. supplication		I.	PLIC-, PLEX-, [-PLY]
____ 10. auspices		J.	PREC-
____ 11. sacristy		K.	SACR-, (SECR-)
____ 12. transmigration		L.	SPEC-, (SPIC-), SPECT-

8. Review: Personal Names. Match each name with its <u>etymological</u> meaning.

____ 1. Adelphe (cf. Philadelphia)	A. defender of men
____ 2. Cosmo	B. of the resurrection
____ 3. Evangeline	C. bearer of victory
____ 4. Georgette	D. good news
____ 5. Isidora	E. dear to God
____ 6. Christopher	F. lover of horses
____ 7. Theophila	G. gift of Isis
____ 8. Alexander	H. sister
____ 9. Jason (IATR-)	I. of the holy name
____ 10. Jerome (= Hieronymus)	J. order
____ 11. Nicodemus	K. well-born
____ 12. Philippa	L. Christ-bearer
____ 13. Bernice	M. victory over the people
____ 14. Eugene	N. healer
____ 15. Anastasia	O. little farmer

9. Optional Latin Review: Personal Names. Match each name with the base from which it derives.

____ 1. Dominic	A. AM-
____ 2. Regina	B. DE-, DIV-
____ 3. Justin	C. DOM(IN)-
____ 4. Luke	D. FID-
____ 5. Amanda	E. GRAT-
____ 6. Faith	F. JUR-, JUST-
____ 7. Valerie	G. LUC-
____ 8. Grace	H. NASC-, NAT-
____ 9. Diana	I. PATR-
____ 10. Constance	J. REG-, (RIG-), RECT-
____ 11. Natalie	K. ST(A)-, STIT-, SIST-
____ 12. Patrick	L. VAL-

NOTE: Students may wish to use library resources to determine the etymological meaning of their first and last names.

LESSON XIII

1. <u>ACR-; HIER-; HYDR-; MEGA(L)-; OLIG-; PATR-; PATRI-; SOPH-; TELE-;</u>
<u>XEN-; ZO-</u>

Match each word with the best definition.

____ 1. acrostic	A. a market condition of few sellers
____ 2. hieratic	B. "wise fool"
____ 3. dehydrated	C. priestly
____ 4. megalomaniac	D. fear of foreigners or strangers
____ 5. megalopolis	E. producing motion in objects without physical means
____ 6. oligopoly	F. deprived of water
____ 7. patriarch	G. carnivorous
____ 8. patriot	H. Patrick Henry, for example
____ 9. sophist	I. person skilled in fallacious reasoning
____ 10. sophomore	J. composition in verse, in which the first letters of each line form a word or phrase
____ 11. telekinetic	K. cross-fertilization
____ 12. telepathy	L. person suffering from delusions of grandeur
____ 13. xenophobia	M. mental communication
____ 14. xenogamy	N. male leader of a clan or family
____ 15. zoophagous	O. populated area embracing several metropolises

2. Indicate whether each statement is true or false by circling T or F.

T F 1. An *acrophobe* is unlikely to pursue a career as a high-wire acrobat.

T F 2. Etymologically, a *prophet* speaks for God.

T F 3. *Hydrophobia* is another name for rabies.

T F 4. The etymology of *Vermont* is "purple mountain."

T F 5. People who are careless or clumsy often suffer from *dropsy*.

T F 6. Etymologically, *zodiac* refers to the imaginary band of animals that encircles the heavens.

T F 7. The term *hieroglyphics* can refer to writing that is difficult to read or to decipher.

T   F   8. *Patristic* and *paternal* mean the same thing.

T   F   9. The word *audiophile* is an example of a hybrid (Latin AUD- + Greek PHIL-).

T   F   10. Animal crackers are *zoomorphic*.

3. For further practice with Greek bases, supply the appropriate word or phrase from the lists below.

<u>MANIAS:</u>   <u>An obsession with</u> . . .

1. bibliomania   _____

2. choreomania   _____

3. cynomania   _____

4. dipsomania   _____

5. entomomania   _____

6. gynemania   _____

7. kleptomania   _____

8. monomania   _____

9. pyromania   _____

10. zoomania   _____

animals	dogs	one thing
birds	drinking	running
books	fire	stealing
dancing	insects	women

PHOBIAS: An abnormal fear of . . .

1. agoraphobia   _____

2. algophobia   _____

3. androphobia   _____

4. claustrophobia   _____

5. gamophobia   _____

6. kinesophobia   _____

7. necrophobia   _____

8. neophobia   _____

9. pyrophobia   _____

10. taphephobia   _____

11. thanatophobia   _____

12. toxicophobia   _____

13. triskaidekaphobia   _____

animals	fire	new things
being buried alive	marriage	open spaces
dead bodies	men	pain
death	movement	poison
doctors	narrow spaces	thirteen

The possibilities for manias and phobias are endless. Using your knowledge of Greek bases, construct others that describe yourself, friends, or relatives. Be as fanciful as you wish.

4. Review: Match each word with the best definition.

_____ 1. pedant

_____ 2. architrave

_____ 3. beta

_____ 4. microbe

_____ 5. chromatics

_____ 6. energetic

_____ 7. glossary

_____ 8. optical

_____ 9. carbohydrate

_____ 10. system

_____ 11. dialect

_____ 12. apologize

_____ 13. pancreas

_____ 14. police

_____ 15. sophism

A. any of a group of chemical compounds that constitute a major animal food group

B. organization

C. false argument

D. gland that secretes digestive enzymes

E. the second brightest star of a constellation

F. a regional variety of language

G. minute life form that causes disease

H. a collection of terms in a special field

I. a force that maintains order

J. to express regret for an error

K. the science of color

L. pertaining to the eye

M. vigorous

N. a molded band around a rectangular opening

O. person who makes an ostentatious show of learning

LESSON XIV

1. -METER, -METRY; -SCOPE

Supply the appropriate word from the list below.

1. a line of poetry with six metrical feet   _____

2. an optical instrument that produces a
   variety of patterns using bits of colored glass   _____

3. an instrument for viewing distant objects   _____

4. an instrument for measuring atmospheric pressure   _____

5. an instrument for marking exact time in music   _____

6. an instrument for viewing small objects   _____

7. perfect proportion   _____

8. an optical instrument for viewing objects
   in an otherwise obstructed field of vision   _____

9. a spiritual overseer   _____

10. circumference of a two-dimensional figure   _____

barometer	meter	periscope
bishop	metronome	symmetry
hexameter	microscope	taximeter
kaleidoscope	perimeter	telescope

2. Words of Interest. Supply the appropriate word from the list below.

	Word	Etymological Meaning	Current Meaning
1.	_____	beautiful voice	keyboard musical instrument with steam whistles
2.	_____	deep sound	a male voice between tenor and bass
3.	_____	large world	the universe as a whole
4.	_____	having equal legs	having two equal sides
5.	_____	the rock	a masculine first name
6.	_____	long (mark)	a symbol placed over a vowel to show that it has a long sound
7.	_____	beautiful strength	gymnastic exercises
8.	_____	rock oil	a fossil fuel
9.	_____	view in every direction	a comprehensive presentation
10.	_____	no place	a place of ideal perfection
11.	_____	beautiful handwriting	elegant penmanship
12.	_____	light-writing	an image produced by a camera
13.	_____	celery rock	herb used as garnish
14.	_____	writings	writings found on walls
15.	_____	occult learning	alluring attractiveness

baritone   graffiti   parsley
calisthenics   isosceles   Peter
calligraphy   macron   petroleum
calliope   macrocosm   photograph
glamour   panorama   utopia

3. <u>-GRAM, -GRAPH</u>

Match each word with the best definition.

____ 1. autobiography	A. penmanship
____ 2. graphic	B. illegal gain
____ 3. graphite	C. a short, often satirical poem
____ 4. graft	D. a person's own life story
____ 5. grammar	E. inadvertent repetition of letters or words in copying
____ 6. epigram	F. a word formed by transposing the letters of another
____ 7. program	G. a plan or schedule
____ 8. anagram	H. inscription
____ 9. chirography	I. lifelike
____ 10. dittography	J. study of the inflection and syntax of a language
	K. soft carbon used in pencils

4. Indicate whether each statement is true or false by circling T or F.

T   F   1. An archaeologist is more likely than most people to encounter *petroglyphs*.

T   F   2. Etymologically, the verb *arrive* means "to reach shore."

T   F   3. *Engrave* ultimately derives from the combining form -GRAPH.

T   F   4. A *photosensitive* person is camera-shy.

T   F   5. *Bandy*, as in the expression "to bandy words," derives from the game of tennis.

T   F   6. The word *juggernaut* (Hindi *jagannath*) has come to mean any large, powerful force that crushes anything in its path.

T   F   7. John D. Rockefeller was renowned for *lycanthropy*.

T   F   8. The etymology of *checkmate* is "the king is dead."

T   F   9. The expression *salad days* refers to the period of life when people are still "green," and hence inexperienced.

T   F   10. An *isobar* is a line on a weather map that connects points of equal pressure.

5. Review: Words with Religious Associations. Match each word with the best definition.

____ 1. neophyte	A. church council
____ 2. anathema	B. universal
____ 3. anthem	C. member of a religious community
____ 4. apotheosize	D. an underground burial chamber
____ 5. apostate	E. curse; denunciation
____ 6. blasphemy	F. rites for public worship
____ 7. catholic	G. to deify
____ 8. cenobite	H. a new convert
____ 9. crypt	I. one of the letters in the New Testament
____ 10. dogma	J. sacrilege
____ 11. epistle	K. Moses, for example
____ 12. liturgy	L. hymn or song of praise
____ 13. synod	M. doctrine
____ 14. prophet	N. person who abandons a previous religious faith
____ 15. allegory	O. expression of human experience by symbolic figures

LESSON XV

1. GON-; LAB-, LEP-, LEM-; MES-; PHRA-; STROPH-

Match each word with the best definition.

_____ 1. polygon	A. disaster
_____ 2. syllable	B. restatement of a passage in another form
_____ 3. narcoleptic	C. inverted word order
_____ 4. epilepsy	D. smallest unit of speech
_____ 5. lemma	E. transitional period of the Stone Age
_____ 6. mesencephalon	F. many-sided figure
_____ 7. Mesolithic	G. circumlocution
_____ 8. Mesopotamia	H. theme or subject
_____ 9. paraphrase	I. ancient land between two rivers
_____ 10. periphrasis	J. midbrain
_____ 11. apostrophe	K. experiencing frequent, uncontrollable attacks of sleep
_____ 12. catastrophe	L. punctuation mark indicating omission of letters
	M. disorder of the central nervous system marked by convulsions

2. **Review:** Match each item with the appropriate description.

_____ 1. medical examiner	A. a misanthrope
_____ 2. "swift-footed" Achilles	B. an avocation
_____ 3. Scrooge	C. an epithet
_____ 4. Amazons	D. an epitaph
_____ 5. Jackson	E. a pseudonym
_____ 6. frog	F. a race of female warriors
_____ 7. philately	G. person who conducts autopsies
_____ 8. New Zealand	H. the antipodes of England
_____ 9. Here lies John Doe	I. an amphibian
_____ 10. Lewis Carroll	J. a patronymic

3. **Optional Latin Review:** Travel. Match each word with the base from which it derives.

____ 1. suitcase	A. AG-, (IG-), ACT-
____ 2. itinerary	B. AQU(A)-
____ 3. train	C. BI-, BIN-
____ 4. agent	D. CRUC-
____ 5. bicycle	E. I-, IT-
____ 6. stagecoach	F. JAC-, JECT-
____ 7. automobile	G. MOV-, MOT-
____ 8. aquaplane	H. MUT-
____ 9. voyage	I. OMNI-
____ 10. commuter	J. SEQU-, SECUT-
____ 11. cruise	K. SERV-
____ 12. bus	L. ST(A)-, STIT-, SIST-
____ 13. reservation	M. TERMIN-
____ 14. jet	N. TRACT-
____ 15. terminal	O. VI(A)-

4. **Optional Latin and Greek Review:** Animals. Match each word with its <u>etymological</u> meaning.

____ 1. dinosaur	A. flame
____ 2. mastiff	B. earth dog
____ 3. terrier	C. river horse
____ 4. mastodon	D. leaper
____ 5. flamingo	E. clear singer
____ 6. canary	F. thick skin
____ 7. hippopotamus	G. fear-inspiring lizard
____ 8. dromedary	H. bone crusher
____ 9. rhinoceros	I. horned nose
____ 10. chanticleer	J. flat foot
____ 11. salmon	K. accustomed to the hand
____ 12. osprey	L. bird from the "Dog Islands"
____ 13. platypus	M. runner
____ 14. pachyderm	N. shadow tail
____ 15. squirrel	O. nipple-shaped tooth

LESSON XVI

1. Match each word with the best definition.

____	1. monocle	A. double vision
____	2. hemiplegia	B. divided into six parts
____	3. diplopia	C. having five digits
____	4. tripod	D. an eyeglass for one eye
____	5. pentadactyl	E. a verse of seven feet
____	6. heptameter	F. having eight parts
____	7. hexamerous	G. a group of four
____	8. octamerous	H. to assume total control of something
____	9. monopolize	I. three-legged stand
____	10. tetrad	J. paralysis of one side of the body

2. Indicate whether each statement is true or false by circling T or F.

T   F   1. Vampires are believed to practice *hematophagy*.

T   F   2. *Hex* (to bewitch) ultimately derives from the base HEX(A)- (six).

T   F   3. The etymological meaning of *pagan* is "infidel."

T   F   4. The word *chiliad* (one thousand) is a synonym for "millennium."

T   F   5. An ancient Roman would have been unfamiliar with the gesture "thumbs down."

T   F   6. The *Decalogue* is a drama both famous and unique in antiquity for its ten speaking parts.

T   F   7. *Attic* originally meant "pertaining to Attica."

T   F   8. *Gymnosophists* (naked philosophers) were ascetic wise men of ancient India who wore little or no clothing.

T   F   9. By extension, the word *octopus* can describe any person or organization with wide-reaching control.

T   F   10. *Miniature* derives from the Latin base MINOR-, MINUS-, MINUT-.

3. Words of Interest. Supply the appropriate word from the list below.

	Word	Etymological Meaning	Current Meaning
1.	_____	ten thousand	a large indefinite number
2.	_____	three folds	set of three hinged panels
3.	_____	situation in which one is seized in two directions	difficult situation
4.	_____	first gluing	diplomatic etiquette
5.	_____	one letter	two or more initials combined into one character
6.	_____	ten contests	contest composed of ten athletic events
7.	_____	every seven days	weekly
8.	_____	place of solitude	place occupied by a religious order
9.	_____	second actor	person who acts as a foil to another
10.	_____	first model	a model on which something is patterned
11.	_____	something with five corners	a five-pointed, star-shaped figure
12.	_____	100 oxen	sacrifice of 100 oxen: any great slaughter
13.	_____	square	tile used in mosaics; token
14.	_____	twofold sheet	document of an educational degree
15.	_____	little table	horizontal bar for acrobatic exercise

decathlon	hecatomb	pentacle
deuteragonist	hyphen	protocol
dichotomy	kilowatt	prototype
dilemma	monastery	tessera
diploma	monogram	trapeze
hebdomadal	myriad	triptych

4. **Review:** From the list below, supply the base(s) or combining form from which each word derives.

1. enthusiasm _____

2. grotto _____

3. amnesty _____

4. boutique _____

5. philter _____

6. ink _____

7. surgery _____

8. ballet _____

9. fancy _____

10. bishop _____

11. glamour _____

12. idiom _____

13. palsy _____

14. blame _____

15. monk _____

16. anthem _____

BALL-, BOL-, BLE-
CAU(S)-
CH(E)IR-
CRYPT-, CRYPH-
ERG-, URG-
-GRAPH, -GRAM
IDI-
LY-
MNE-

MON-
PHA(N)-
PHE(M)-, PHA-
PHIL-
PHON-
-SCOPE
THE- (god)
THE- (to place)

5. **Optional Latin Review:** Supply the missing letters to form an Anglo-Saxon equivalent of each Latinate word.

1. premonition   fore _ _ _ _ ing

2. altitude   h _ _ _ _ _

3. innate   in _ _ _ _

4. regal   k _ _ _ ly

5. flex   b _ _ _

6. immortal   d _ _ _ _ less

7. gratitude   t _ _ _ _ fullness

8. oration   s _ _ _ _ _

9. manual   _ _ _ _ book

10. decapitate   be _ _ _ _

6. **Optional Latin and Greek Review:** Plants. Match each word with its <u>etymological</u> meaning.

____ 1. aster	A. gold flower
____ 2. gladiolus	B. a flower that never grows old
____ 3. cyclamen	C. tree-loving
____ 4. rhododendron	D. of the liver (three-lobed plant)
____ 5. nasturtium	E. water cup
____ 6. ageratum	F. pensive
____ 7. pansy	G. circle
____ 8. heliotrope	H. flesh-colored flower
____ 9. philodendron	I. star
____ 10. hydrangea	J. turning with the sun
____ 11. eglantine	K. nose twister
____ 12. chrysanthemum	L. little sword
____ 13. carnation	M. prickly
____ 14. hepatica	N. lily flower
____ 15. fleur-de-lis	O. rose tree

LESSONS XVII, XVIII, & XIX

1. Match each word with the best definition.

____ 1. choreographer	A. "group of small islands"
____ 2. glyph	B. pedagogy
____ 3. Polynesia	C. relating to navigation or ships
____ 4. Micronesia	D. itinerant
____ 5. erotic	E. composer of dances
____ 6. nautical	F. "group of many islands"
____ 7. aeronautics	G. political dominance of one nation
____ 8. plethora	H. person who practices extreme self-discipline
____ 9. bucolic	I. a carving in relief
____ 10. didactics	J. characterized by pleasure
____ 11. hedonic	K. superfluity
____ 12. paroxysm	L. sudden, violent emotion
____ 13. hegemony	M. pastoral
____ 14. peripatetic	N. pertaining to sexual love
____ 15. ascetic	O. art of flight

2. Indicate whether the following words are singular or plural by circling S or PL.

S	PL	1.	analysis
S	PL	2.	criteria
S	PL	3.	dilemma
S	PL	4.	epitome
S	PL	5.	hoi polloi
S	PL	6.	phenomena
S	PL	7.	metamorphoses
S	PL	8.	thesauri
S	PL	9.	odea
S	PL	10.	phalanx

3. Words of Interest. Supply the appropriate word from the list below.

	Word	Etymological Meaning	Current Meaning
1.	_____	seasickness	queasiness
2.	_____	dog's tail	attention getter
3.	_____	a wound	psychic disorder caused by injury
4.	_____	hostile speech	controversial argument
5.	_____	stain; pollution	a noxious atmosphere
6.	_____	turning like oxen in plowing	alternate lines written from left to right and from right to left
7.	_____	riddle	something difficult to understand
8.	_____	depth	anticlimax; sentimentalism
9.	_____	fixed point	memorable date; extended period of time
10.	_____	instrument made of ox horn	a brass wind instrument
11.	_____	flood	violent upheaval
12.	_____	gigantic statue	amphitheater
13.	_____	mixing bowl	hole; depression in the earth
14.	_____	brand; tattoo	mark of shame
15.	_____	excessiveness	redundancy

bathos	crater	nausea
boustrophedon	cynosure	pleonasm
bugle	enigma	polemic
cataclysm	epoch	stigma
colosseum	miasma	trauma

4. Indicate whether each statement is true or false by circling T or F.

T F 1. The word *martyr* originally meant "witness."

T F 2. Etymologically, the word *belfry* has nothing to do with bells or bell towers.

T F 3. In ancient Rome, as in our own times, applause signified enthusiastic acclamation of a theatrical performance.

T F 4. The word *amnesia* belongs to the NES- (island) family of words.

T F 5. The words *dicker* and *dime* derive from different Latin bases.

T F 6. *Siderodromophobia* means "morbid fear of unidentified flying objects."

T F 7. *Swan song* acquires its present meaning from the once held notion that swans, sensing the approach of death, burst into melodious song.

T F 8. *Eros* is the Greek god of love.

T F 9. Some loan words, such as *hors d'oeuvre*, never completely become English.

T F 10. The word *scene* originally referred to a tent used by Greek actors as a dressing room.

5. Review: Indicate the correct answer by circling A or B.

1. identification of a disease: (A) prognosis (B) diagnosis

2. humorous story: (A) anecdote (B) antidote

3. vivid: (A) graphite (B) graphic

4. married to two persons simultaneously: (A) bigamous (B) digamous

5. formal debate: (A) parlance (B) parry

6. nutritional: (A) tropic (B) trophic

7. shapeless: (A) amorphous   (B) amorous

8. person sensitive to the beautiful: (A) aesthete   (B) athlete

9. theatrical performance: (A) hysterics   (B) histrionics

10. sacrifice of many victims: (A) hector   (B) hecatomb

11. concert hall: (A) odeum   (B) odium

12. biting: (A) caustic   (B) caudal

13. indifference: (A) apathy   (B) empathy

14. producing fever: (A) pyrrhic   (B) pyretic

15. inscription on a tomb: (A) epitaph   (B) epithet

16. science dealing with the eyes: (A) ophiology   (B) ophthalmology

17. to curse: (A) anesthetize   (B) anathematize

18. to predict: (A) procrastinate   (B) prognosticate

19. widespread: (A) endemic   (B) pandemic

20. emblem: (A) allegory   (B) allegiance

6. Optional Latin Review: Match each Latin word or phrase with the best definition.

_____ 1. facsimile   A. greatest work of an artist
_____ 2. memorandum   B. authorization
_____ 3. animus   C. "to whose advantage"
_____ 4. fiat   D. to a sickening degree
_____ 5. cui bono   E. for the time being
_____ 6. per diem   F. hostility
_____ 7. magnum opus   G. reproduction
_____ 8. pro tempore   H. with academic distinction
_____ 9. ad nauseam   I. a written reminder
_____ 10. cum laude   J. for each day

REVIEW OF LESSONS XII-XIX (SELF-TESTING: Answers can be found in Appendix C.)

1. Match each word with the best definition.

_____ 1. metempsychosis	A. paralyzed with fear
_____ 2. automatic	B. similar
_____ 3. ideogram	C. transmigration of the soul
_____ 4. petrified	D. spontaneous
_____ 5. hydrophilic	E. having a strong affinity for water
_____ 6. ego trip	F. inflammation of the stomach
_____ 7. parallel	G. witchcraft
_____ 8. gastritis	H. a written symbol, such as & or =
_____ 9. hierarchy	I. project undertaken principally to satisfy one's self-image
_____ 10. necromancy	J. group of persons organized according to rank

2. Indicate whether each statement is true or false by circling T or F.

T   F   1. *Explode* owes its origin to the Roman theater, where the audience indicated its displeasure by "clapping the actor off the stage."

T   F   2. Picky eaters might be termed *oligophagous*.

T   F   3. The name of the flower *zinnia* ultimately derives from the base XEN-.

T   F   4. Etymologically, *Mediterranean* and *Mesopotamia* describe places situated between land or water.

T   F   5. *Paragon* derives from the base GON-.

T   F   6. *Octopus* admits two plurals, "octopuses" and "octopi."

T   F   7. The etymology of *impersonate* is "to put on another's mask."

T   F   8. *Glamour* originally referred to occult learning.

T   F   9. The expression "to tide us over" derives from the sport of sailboat racing.

T   F   10. In Norman England the word *ignoramus* meant "victim."

T   F   11. *Bucolic* derives from the Greek word for cow.

T   F   12. *Salary*, *sausage*, and *salad* all come from the Latin base for salt.

T   F   13. The *Colosseum* in Rome derived its name from its proximity to an enormous statue of the emperor Nero.

T   F   14. The etymology of *brand-new* is "fresh from the blacksmith's fire."

T   F   15. *Squire* originally referred to a knight's shield bearer.

3. Words of Interest. Supply the appropriate word from the list below.

	Word	Etymological Meaning	Current Meaning
1.	_____	solitary person	male member of a religious community
2.	_____	a turning back of the enemy	a prize for victory or achievement
3.	_____	six threads	heavy medieval silk fabric
4.	_____	small animal figure	an imaginary belt of constellations
5.	_____	a commonplace	subject; theme
6.	_____	beautiful old age	monk of the eastern church
7.	_____	hour observer	astrological prediction
8.	_____	taken together	unit of spoken speech
9.	_____	seasickness	loud or unpleasant sound
10.	_____	choral dance	company of singers

callipygian   monk   syllable
caloyer   noise   topic
choir   saltpeter   trophy
horoscope   samite   zodiac

246

4. By combining Greek elements, form English words with the following meanings.

1. rule by one _____

2. the writing of one's own life story _____

3. worship of the dead _____

4. a lover of the French _____

5. fear of being buried alive _____

6. person obsessed with self _____

7. scientist who studies celestial phenomena _____

8. irrational fear of heights _____

9. an instrument that can view small objects _____

10. the study of human lives and cultures _____

5. Identify the numerical base(s) in each word and then give the meanings of the bases.

1. hectograph _____

2. triad _____

3. kilogram _____

4. heptarchy _____

5. protein _____

6. pentameter _____

7. dilemma _____

8. triskaidekaphobia _____

9. dichotomize _____

10. monocle _____

6. Match each word with the best definition.

____ 1. pseudo	A. the common people
____ 2. barometer	B. growing toward or away from the light
____ 3. telegnosis	C. in a drama, the final resolution of the plot
____ 4. dilemma	D. plausible but false reasoning
____ 5. diorama	E. a mark of punctuation (-)
____ 6. sophistry	F. wisdom
____ 7. chorea	G. clairvoyance
____ 8. catastrophe	H. to reword
____ 9. glyptic	I. equality of political rights
____ 10. phototropic	J. scene reproduced in three dimensions
____ 11. paraphrase	K. false; pretended
____ 12. isonomy	L. knowledge acquired through travel abroad
____ 13. hyphen	M. disease of the nervous system
____ 14. encomium	N. a formal expression of praise
____ 15. hoi polloi	O. pertaining to carving
	P. instrument that measures atmospheric pressure
	Q. a difficult problem

7. Supply the missing prefix or base to form the <u>antonym</u> of each of word.

1. neolithic   _ _ _ _ olithic

2. microcephalic   _ _ _ _ cephalic

3. cacography   _ _ _ _ igraphy

4. perihelion   _ _ helion

5. macrocosm   _ _ _ _ ocosm

Name _____

GREEK REVIEW (LESSONS III-XIX) (SELF-TESTING: Answers can be found in Appendix C.)

1. Match each word with the best definition.

_____ 1. gastronome	A. first martyr in any cause
_____ 2. hematogenous	B. worship of images
_____ 3. thaumaturgy	C. intended for general circulation
_____ 4. iconolatry	D. petrified plant
_____ 5. psychiatrist	E. gourmet
_____ 6. protomartyr	F. self-taught
_____ 7. ethnocentricism	G. rule by the few
_____ 8. autodidactic	H. magic
_____ 9. dendrolite	I. physician who treats mental disorders
_____ 10. parallel	J. dentist who straightens teeth
_____ 11. oligarchy	K. similar
_____ 12. baroscope	L. producing blood
_____ 13. egomaniacal	M. extremely self-centered
_____ 14. orthodontist	N. instrument that indicates variations in pressure on the same line
_____ 15. encyclical	O. belief in the superiority of one's own culture

2. Indicate whether each statement is true or false by circling T or F.

T F 1. A cell with a "fondness for acids" creates *acidophilus* milk.

T F 2. A *decathlon* refers to a contest consisting of seven athletic events.

T F 3. The etymology of *bulimia* is "hunger of an ox."

T F 4. A person who dates only foreigners may be described as a *xenophile*.

T F 5. The French *adieu* and the Spanish *adios* are roughly equivalent to the English *good-bye*.

T F 6. *Criticaster* is composed of two Greek bases, CRI- and AST(E)R-.

T F 7. *Peculiar* derives from the Latin word for cattle (*pecus*).

T F 8. *Ruminate* originally meant "to chew the cud."

T   F   9. *Anthem* and *antiphon* can both refer to a hymn sung in alternate parts.

T   F   10. *George* is a particularly appropriate name for a farmer.

3. Words of Interest. Supply the appropriate word from the list below.

	Word	Etymological Meaning	Current Meaning
1.	_____	stitching of songs	musical composition of irregular form
2.	_____	instrument for viewing shapes	a constantly changing set of colors or beautiful patterns
3.	_____	slanderer	Satan
4.	_____	new growth	beginner
5.	_____	a person's word	conditional release of a prisoner
6.	_____	a private citizen	foolish person
7.	_____	full armor	a complete array
8.	_____	matters of arrangement	maneuvers for gaining success
9.	_____	all imitation	the telling of a story through body movements only
10.	_____	chief sea	expanse of water with scattered islands
11.	_____	tube	mounted gun
12.	_____	pedestal; balcony	a bench in a church

archipelago	kaleidoscope	parole
cannon	neophyte	pew
devil	panoply	rhapsody
idiot	pantomime	tactics

4. Match each Latin-based word with its Greek-based synonym.

_____ 1. obituary	A. epistle
_____ 2. lunatic	B. mantic
_____ 3. division	C. anomalous
_____ 4. irregular	D. schism
_____ 5. transcendental	E. agonizing
_____ 6. similar	F. pyretic
_____ 7. missive	G. maniac
_____ 8. divinatory	H. necrology
_____ 9. febrile	I. analogous
_____ 10. excruciating	J. metaphysical

5. Supply the missing base.

1. empty tomb	ceno _ _ _ _
2. pain of longing for things past	nost _ _ _ ia
3. having good digestion	eu _ _ _ _ ic
4. a false or assumed name	_ _ _ _ _ onym
5. a diacritical mark that indicates a long sound	_ _ _ _ on
6. pertaining to sight	_ _ _ ical
7. a mentally disturbed person with delusions of greatness	_ _ _ _ _ omaniac
8. study of form and structure	_ _ _ _ _ ology

9. holding a different opinion   _ _ _ _ _ odoxical

10. composed of the same kind of parts   _ _ _ ogeneous

11. science of colors   _ _ _ _ _ _ _ ics

12. person who can speak three   tri _ _ _ _
    languages

13. extrasensory perception   _ _ _ _ pathy

14. world in miniature   micro _ _ _ _

15. study of ancient writing   _ _ _ _ ography

16. first or original model   _ _ _ _ otype

17. contest of ten athletic events   _ _ _ athlon

18. woman hater   _ _ _ ogynist

19. birth of the gods   _ _ _ ogony

20. lover of human beings   _ _ _ _ anthrope

6. Words of Interest. Supply the appropriate word from the list below.

1. Egyptian writing   _____

2. something remarkable or unusual   _____

3. powerful explosive used for blasting _____

4. water clock   _____

5. a specialty shop   _____

6. ancient two-handled vessel   _____

7. song of praise   _____

8. model of excellence   _____

9. art of improving the memory   _____

10. place were official records are kept   _____

11. beautifying   _____

12. anticipatory   _____

amphora	clepsydra	mnemonics
anthem	cosmetic	paragon
archives	dynamite	phenomenon
boutique	hieroglyphics	proleptic

7. Match each Greek-based word with its Latin-based equivalent.

____ 1. diathesis   A. omniscient

____ 2. apathetic   B. amorous

____ 3. epigraph   C. disposition

____ 4. nautical   D. quadrangular

____ 5. pansophic   E. insectivorous

____ 6. tetragonal   F. bisectional

____ 7. polyanthous   G. inscription

____ 8. erotic   H. multiflorous

____ 9. dichotomous   I. impassive

____ 10. entomophagous   J. naval

8. Identify the prefix (if any) and base(s) in each word and give the meaning of each element. Then indicate whether the word is a noun, an adjective, or a verb by circling N, A, or V.

MEANINGS

1. dyslexia _____ N A V

2. aphelion _____ N A V

3. Catholicism _____ N A V

4. evangelize _____ N A V

5. pedagogics _____ N A V

6. perigee _____ N A V

7. paradoxical _____ N A V

8. asterisk _____ N A V

9. stereotypic _____ N A V

10. prognosticate _____ N A V

11. epidermal _____ N A V

12. demonic _____ N A V

13. polygamous _____ N A V

14. cinema _____ N A V

15. empathy _____ N A V

16. antiphrasis _____ N A V

17. politician _____ N A V

18. anonymous   _____   N A V

19. cataclysm   _____   N A V

20. podium   _____   N A V

9. Match each Greek-based word with its Latin-based synonym.

____ 1. caustic	A. transitory
____ 2. peripatetic	B. resuscitation
____ 3. trophic	C. palmistry
____ 4. anabiosis	D. nutritive
____ 5. chronic	E. itinerant
____ 6. chiromancy	F. library
____ 7. tautology	G. redundancy
____ 8. ephemeral	H. celestial
____ 9. bibliotheca	I. habitual
____ 10. ethereal	J. mordant

APPENDIXES

APPENDIX A

ASSIMILATION OF PREFIXES

Assimilation refers to a modification in the basic form of a prefix that results when the prefix is added to a base. In this process, which was occurring even in Roman times, certain speech sounds blend to become similar or identical (example: ad + NUL- > annul). Assimilation is likely to occur when a prefix ending in a consonant comes before a base beginning with a consonant. This phonetic change typically results in a word that is easier to pronounce and sounds more pleasing to the ear. See for yourself in the examples below.

The Latin prefixes that regularly undergo assimilation include: AD-, CON-, DIS-, EX-, IN-, OB, and SUB-. Note that the prefix ab-, a-, abs- (away, from) is <u>never</u> assimilated.

<u>There are three kinds of assimilation:</u>

1. The last letter of the prefix becomes the same as the first letter of the base.

a. ad	+	gression	→	aggression (instead of adgression)
b. con	+	lude	→	collude (instead of conlude)
c. ob	+	fer	→	offer (instead of obfer)
d. in	+	luminate	→	illuminate (instead of inluminate)
e. con	+	roborate	→	corroborate (instead of conroborate)

2. The last letter of the prefix changes to a different letter that sounds more harmonious with the first letter of the base.

a. in	+	part	→	impart (instead of inpart)
b. con	+	punction	→	compunction (instead of conpunction)
c. sub	+	tenance	→	sustenance (instead of subtenance)
d. ad	+	quire	→	acquire (instead of adquire)

3. The last letter of the prefix drops out altogether.

a. ad	+	venue	→	avenue (instead of advenue)
b. con	+	habit	→	cohabit (instead of conhabit)
c. dis	+	verse	→	diverse (instead of disverse)
d. ex	+	lude	→	elude (instead of exlude)

APPENDIX B

LATIN AND GREEK EQUIVALENTS

The following list of Latin and Greek equivalents is not intended to be exhaustive but does contain a number of the more important prefixes and bases introduced in *English Words from Latin and Greek Elements.*

Prefixes

Latin	Greek	Meaning
ab-, a-, abs-	apo-, ap-	from; away from
ambi-	amphi-	both; around
con-, com-	syn-, sym-	with
dis-, di-	dia-, di-	asunder; apart
ex-, e-	ec-, ex-	out; out of
extra-, extro-	exo-, ecto-	outside
in-, im-	en-, em-	in; into
intra-, intro-	endo-, ento-	within
pre-/pro-	pro-	before; in front of
sub-	hypo-, hyp-	below
super-	hyper-	over

Appendix B

Bases

Latin	Greek	Meaning
AC(U)-, ACR-, ACET-	ACR-	a point
AG-, (IG-), ACT-	-AGOG(UE)	to lead
ART-	ARTHR-	art; joint
AUD-	AESTHE-, ESTHE-	to hear; to perceive
BI-, BIN-	DI-, DIPL-	two; twice
CAPIT-, (CIPIT-)	CEPHAL-	head
CENT-	HECT-	a hundred
CERN-, CRET-	CRI-	to decide; to judge
CORD-	CARDI-	heart
DECEM-; DECI(M)-	DEC(A)-	ten; tenth
DOC-, DOCT-	DOX-, DOG-	to teach; teaching
DU-	DICH-	(in) two
EGO-	EGO-	I
FA(B)-, FAT-, FESS-, FAM-	PHE(M)-, PHA-	to say
FER-	PHER-, PHOR-	to bear
FOLI-	PHYLL-	leaf
GEN-/NASC-, NAT-	GEN(E)-, GON-	to produce
GENER-, GEN-	GEN(E)-	race; kind
GNO-, NO-, NOT-	GNO(S)-	to know
GRAV-	BAR-	heavy; weight

Appendix B

Latin	Greek	Meaning
LEG-, (LIG-), LECT-	LOG-, [-LOGUE], LECT-	to pick; to read
LUC-, LUMIN-	LEUC-, LEUK-	light; white
MAGN-	MEGA(L)-	great; large
MEDI-	MES-	middle
MILL-	KILO-	a thousand
MON-	MNE-	to warn; to remember
NOC-, NOX-, NIC-, NEC-	NECR-	to kill; corpse
NOMEN-, NOMIM-	ONYM-	name
NOV-	NE-	new
NOVEM-; NON-	ENNEA-	nine; ninth
OCT-; OCTAV-	OCT(A)-	eight; eighth
PATI-, PASS-	PATH-	to feel; to suffer
PATR-, PATERN-	PATR-	father
PED-	POD-	foot
PRIM-	PROT-	first
QUINQUE-; QUINT-	PENT(A)-	five; fifth
RAP-, RAPT-, (REPT-)	LAB-, LEP-, LEM-	to seize
SCI-	SCHIZ-, SCHIS-	to know (to separate one from another)
SEMI-	HEMI-	half
SEPT(EM)-, SEPTIM-	HEPT(A)-	seven; seventh
SEX-; SEXT-	HEX(A)-	six; sixth
SIMIL-, SIMUL-	HOM(E)-	the same

Latin	Greek	Meaning
SOLV-, SOLUT-	LY-	to loosen
SPEC-, (SPIC-), SPECT-	-SCOPE	to see
ST(A)-, STIT-, SIST-	STA-	to stand
TEND-, TENT-, TENS-	TON(US)-	to stretch
TRI-; TERTI-	TRI-	three; third
UND-	HYDR-	wave; water
VID-, VIS-	IDE-	to see; object of vision
VIV-	BI-	to live; life

APPENDIX C

ANSWERS TO MAJOR REVIEW SECTIONS

PART I: WORD ELEMENTS FROM LATIN

Review of Lessons II–VII (pp. 41–44)

1. 1–ad; 2–sub; 3–con; 4–ex; 5–dis; 6–in; 7–ad; 8–in; 9–ob; 10–sub.

2. 1–de; 2–se; 3–ab; 4–pro; 5–circum; 6–post; 7–extro; 8–inter; 9–ad; 10–di; 11–super; 12–col; 13–intro; 14–trans; 15–per.

3. 1–June; 2–March; 3–December; 4–January; 5–April; 6–February; 7–October; 8–July; 9–September; 10–August.

4. 1–D; 2–J; 3–C; 4–G; 5–I; 6–B; 7–F; 8–H; 9–E; 10–A.

5. 1–PRIM; 2–LOQU; 3–UN; 4–JUR; 5–ENNI; 6–VOC; 7–ALIEN; 8–DU; 9–MALE; 10–PART; 11–VERB; 12–MULT; 13–PED; 14–SANCT; 15–MAGN; 16–SENS; 17–PEND; 18–PLEN; 19–ANIM; 20–CANT.

6. 1–A; 2–B; 3–B; 4–B; 5–B; 6–B; 7–A; 8–A; 9–B; 10–A; 11–B; 12–A.

7. 1–S; 2–A; 3–S; 4–A; 5–S; 6–A; 7–S; 8–A; 9–S; 10–S; 11–S; 12–S; 13–S; 14–A; 15–S.

Review of Lessons VIII–XIV (pp. 85–88)

1. 1–F; 2–T; 3–F; 4–F; 5–T; 6–T; 7–F; 8–T; 9–F; 10–T; 11–T; 12–T; 13–T; 14–F; 15–F.

2. 1–C; 2–E; 3–D; 4–A; 5–B.

3. 1–S; 2–S; 3–S; 4–A; 5–A; 6–A; 7–S; 8–S; 9–S; 10–S; 11–S; 12–S; 13–S; 14–A; 15–S.

4. 1–L; 2–N; 3–K; 4–M; 5–D; 6–J; 7–F; 8–A; 9–G; 10–B; 11–O; 12–I; 13–E; 14–H; 15–C.

5. 1–NAT; 2–CAPT; 3–DIV; 4–NOV; 5–CRED; 6–VER; 7–OR; 8–LATER; 9–LUMIN; 10–MUT; 11–PULS; 12–(P)OSIT; 13–AM; 14–SIMIL; 15–FA; 16–CORPOR; 17–FLAT; 18–FOLI; 19–DUR; 20–(F)ACT.

6. 1–E; 2–L; 3–H; 4–B; 5–M; 6–I; 7–C; 8–F; 9–O; 10–N; 11–J; 12–D; 13–K; 14–G; 15–A.

Appendix C

Review of Lessons XV–XIX (pp. 115–118)

1. 1–T; 2–T; 3–F; 4–T; 5–T; 6–T; 7–F; 8–F; 9–F; 10–T; 11–T; 12–T; 13–T; 14–T; 15–F.

2. 1–SCRIPT; 2–VIV; 3–(M)ATER; 4–NOMIN; 5–DICT; 6–VAL; 7–SCI; 8–FRANG; 9–SON; 10–(S)CRIB; 11–(M)INUT; 12–CRES; 13–SOL; 14–PATRI; 15–MON.

3. 1–D; 2–J; 3–A; 4–G; 5–F; 6–B; 7–H, 8–C; 9–E; 10–I.

4. 1–S; 2–A; 3–S; 4–A; 5–A; 6–S; 7–S; 8–S; 9–S; 10–S; 11–S; 12–S; 13–A; 14–A; 15–A.

5. 1–before, in front of + send, let go; 2–apart, in different directions, not + sound; 3–out, from, completely + follow; 4–both, around + be strong, be worth; 5–cry out; 6–to, toward + grow; 7–in, into, against, not + seek, ask; 8–do, drive; 9–grain; 10–live; 11–father; 12–around + stand; 13–warn, advise; 14–forward, in front of, for + throw; 15–cut; 16–small, smaller; 17–toward, against, completely + go; 18–with, together, very + endure, suffer; 19–back, again + to roll; 20–break.

Review of Lessons XX–XXV (pp. 149–154)

1. 1–advertisement; 2–automobile; 3–blitzkrieg; 4–fanatic(al); 5–disport; 6–periwig.

2. 1–corrigenda; 2–nostrum; 3–agenda; 4–pace; 5–imprimatur; 6–via; 7–memento; 8–genus; 9–animus; 10–minutiae; 11–succubus; 12–decorum; 13–finis; 14–facsimile; 15–credo.

3. 1–B; 2–B; 3–A; 4–B; 5–A; 6–C; 7–C; 8–A.

4. 1–MORT; 2–AUD; 3–GRAT; 4–PET; 5–RADIC; 6–CORD; 7–LOC; 8–ALT; 9–MANU; 10–CAPIT; 11–(F)LEX; 12–SPIR; 13–CARN; 14–GNO; 15–VICT; 16–MOV; 17–AL; 18–VULG; 19–PUG; 20–SAT.

5. 1–F; 2–F; 3–F; 4–T; 5–T; 6–T; 7–T; 8–T; 9–F; 10–T; 11–T; 12–T; 13–T; 14–T; 15–F.

6. 1–K; 2–H; 3–C; 4–D; 5–A; 6–I; 7–N; 8–L; 9–B; 10–E; 11–M; 12–F.

7. 1–C; 2–A; 3–C; 4–B; 5–A.

8. 1–CAPIT, (CIPIT); 2–LOC; 3–PUT; 4–SPIR; 5–MISC, MIXT; 6–STRU, STRUCT; 7–AL, ALT; 8–AUD; 9–MOV, MOT; 10–GRAT; 11–PORT; 12–MORT-; 13–CORD; 14–NUNCI; 15–MAN(U).

10. 1–J; 2–G; 3–D; 4–A; 5–F; 6–I; 7–B; 8–H; 9–C; 10–E.

11. 1–A; 2–S; 3–S; 4–S; 5–A; 6–A; 7–S; 8–A; 9–S; 10–A.

Appendix C

Latin Review (Lessons II–XXV) (pp. 155–161)

1. 1–F; 2–T; 3–F; 4–T; 5–T; 6–T; 7–T; 8–F; 9–T; 10–T; 11–F; 12–F; 13–T; 14–T; 15–T.

2. 1–VIS; 2–COG; 3–TERR; 4–FACT; 5–PATRI; 6–MUT; 7–SCRIB; 8–MULT; 9–CARN; 10–MILL; 11–AUD; 12–FIN; 13–DICT; 14–LOC; 15–LINE.

3. 1–C; 2–A; 3–B; 4–C; 5–B; 6–B; 7–A; 8–C; 9–B; 10–A; 11–A; 12–B; 13–C; 14–A; 15–B; 16–A; 17–C; 18–B; 19–C; 20–A; 21–B; 22–A; 23–C; 24–B; 25–A.

4. 1–con 2–de; 3–op; 4–dis; 5–suf; 6–con; 7–pro; 8–ex.

5. 1–B; 2–D; 3–J; 4–A; 5–I; 6–C; 7–K; 8–L; 9–E; 10–F; 11–H; 12–G.

6. 1 and 4; 3; 1, 3, and 4; 2 and 4.

7. 1–L; 2–C; 3–A; 4–H; 5–B; 6–F; 7–O; 8–N; 9–J; 10–E; 11–M; 12–D; 13–I; 14–G; 15–K.

8. 1–S; 2–S; 3–S; 4–A; 5–A; 6–A; 7–A; 8–A; 9–S; 10–A; 11–S; 12–S; 13–S; 14–S; 15–S.

9. 1–L; 2–E; 3–J; 4–I; 5–H; 6–M; 7–A; 8–O; 9–F; 10–N; 11–D; 12–K; 13–C; 14–B; 15–G.

10. 1, 3, and 4; 1; 1, 3, and 4.

11. 1–ab + UND, A; 2–a + PART, N; 3–AQUA, N; 4–circum + FER, N; 5–cor + RIG, N; 6–de + FAM, N; 7–ef + FERV, V; 8–en + DUR, N; 9–ex + (S)ECUT, N; 10–extra + SENS, A; 11–im + MIGR, V; 12–LAT, N; 13–LECT, N; 14–per + TIN, A; 15–pre + CURS, N; 16–RAP, A; 17–SAL, A; 18–super + FLU, N; 19–TURB, A; 20–VER, V.

PART II: WORD ELEMENTS FROM GREEK

Review of Lessons I–VI (pp. 189–192)

1. 1–synonym; 2–ectoderm; 3–euphoria; 4–hypotrophy; 5–eulogistic; 6–endomorph; 7–hyperglycemia; 8–cathode; 9–dystrophy; 10–anabasis.

2. 1–D; 2–A; 3–E; 4–H; 5–G; 6–B.

3. 1–podagra; 2–amnesty; 3–nostalgia; 4–pandemonium; 5–apocrypha; 6–palinode; 7–hyperbole; 8–panacea; 9–tome; 10–paraphernalia; 11–iconoclast; 12–canister; 13–enthusiasm; 14–tragedy; 15–democracy.

4. 1–A; 2–A; 3–S; 4–A; 5–S; 6–A; 7–A; 8–A; 9–S; 10–S; 11–S; 12–S; 13–S; 14–A; 15–S.

5. 1–F; 2–F; 3–T; 4–T; 5–F; 6–T; 7–T; 8–F; 9–T; 10–F.

6. 1–F; 2–P; 3–J; 4–A; 5–D; 6–Q; 7–C; 8–M; 9–G; 10–B; 11–O; 12–E; 13–N; 14–L; 15–H.

Review of Lessons VII–XI (pp. 217–219)

1. 1–C; 2–E; 3–I; 4–A; 5–F; 6–H; 7–D; 8–J; 9–G; 10–B.

2. 1–hyp; 2–HETER; 3–dys; 4–PHIL; 5–POLY; 6–ORTH; 7–sym; 8–ANDR; 9–CAC; 10–epi.

3. 1–PHON, N; 2–GER, IATR, A; 3–TECHN, A; 4–hyper, KINE, N; 5–NE, PHY, N; 6–MIS, GYN, N; 7–hypo, CRI, N; 8–OPT, N; 9–COSM, POL, N; 10–em, BLE, A; 11–pro, GNOS, N; 12–ana, THE, N; 13–AESTHE, N; 14–ASTR, A; 15–eu, PHEM, N; 16–SCHIZ, GEN, A; 17–ex, ODONT, N; 18–apo, STA, N; 19–em, PHA, A; 20–DYN, N.

4. 1–H; 2–L; 3–J; 4–A; 5–G; 6–E; 7–K; 8–F; 9–B; 10–C.

5. 1–T; 2–F; 3–F; 4–T; 5–T; 6–T; 7–T; 8–T; 9–F; 10–F.

Review of Lessons XII–XIX (pp. 245–248)

1. 1–C; 2–D; 3–H; 4–A; 5–E; 6–I; 7–B; 8–F; 9–J; 10–G.

2. 1–T; 2–T; 3–F; 4–T; 5–F; 6–T; 7–T; 8–T; 9–F; 10–F; 11–T; 12–T; 13–T; 14–T; 15–T.

3. 1–monk; 2–trophy; 3–samite; 4–zodiac; 5–topic; 6–caloyer; 7–horoscope; 8–syllable; 9–noise; 10–choir.

4. 1–monarchy; 2–autobiography; 3–necrolatry; 4–Francophile; 5–taphephobia; 6–egomaniac; 7–astronomer; 8–acrophobia; 9–microscope; 10–anthropology.

5. 1–HECT, a hundred; 2–TRI, three; 3–KILO, one thousand; 4–HEPT, seven; 5–PROT, first; 6–PENTA, five; 7–DI, two; 8–TRI[S] DEKA, three, ten; 9–DICH, in two; 10–MON, one, single.

6. 1–K; 2–P; 3–G; 4–Q; 5–J; 6–D; 7–M; 8–C; 9–O; 10–B; 11–H; 12–I; 13–E; 14–N; 15–A.

7. 1–PALE; 2–MEGA; 3–CALL; 4–ap; 5–MICR.

Appendix C

Greek Review (Lessons III–XIX) (pp.249–255)

1. 1–E; 2–L; 3–H; 4–B; 5–I; 6–A; 7–O; 8–F; 9–D; 10–K;11–G; 12–N; 13–M; 14–J; 15–C.

2. 1–T; 2–F; 3–T; 4–T; 5–T; 6–F; 7–T; 8–T; 9–T; 10–T.

3. 1–rhapsody; 2–kaleidoscope; 3–devil; 4–neophyte; 5–parole; 6–idiot; 7–panoply; 8–tactics; 9–pantomime; 10–archipelago; 11–cannon; 12–pew.

4. 1–H; 2–G; 3–D; 4–C; 5–J; 6–I; 7–A; 8–B; 9–F; 10–E.

5. 1–TAPH; 2–ALG; 3–PEPT; 4–PSEUD; 5–MACR; 6–OPT; 7–MEGAL; 8–MORPH; 9–HETER; 10–HOM; 11–CHROMAT; 12–GLOT; 13–TELE; 14–COSM; 15–PALE; 16–PROT; 17–DEC; 18–MIS; 19–THE; 20–PHIL.

6. 1–hieroglyphics; 2–phenomenon; 3–dynamite; 4–clepsydra; 5–boutique; 6–amphora; 7–anthem; 8–paragon; 9–mnemonics; 10–archives; 11–cosmetic; 12–proleptic.

7. 1–C; 2–I; 3–G; 4–J; 5–A; 6–D; 7–H; 8–B; 9–F; 10–E.

8. 1–dys, LEX, N; 2–ap, HELI, N; 3–cat, HOL, N; 4–ev, ANGEL, V; 5–PED, AGOG, N; 6–peri, GE, N; 7–para DOX, A; 8–ASTER, N; 9–STERE, TYP, A; 10–pro, GNOS, V; 11–epi, DERM, A; 12–DEMON, A; 13–POLY, GAM, A; 14–CINE, N; 15–em, PATH, N; 16–anti, PHRA, N; 17–POL, N; 18–an, ONYM, A; 19–cata, CLYS, N; 20–POD, N.

9. 1–J; 2–E; 3–D; 4–B; 5–I; 6–C; 7–G; 8–A; 9–F; 10–H.